From Warism to Pacifism

A Moral Continuum

From Warism to Pacifism

A Moral Continuum

Duane L. Cady

Temple University Press
Philadelphia

Temple University Press, Philadelphia 19122
Copyright © 1989 by Temple University. All rights reserved
Published 1989
Printed in the United States of America

Library of Congress Cataloging-in-Publication Data

Cady, Duane L.
From warism to pacifism.

Bibliography: p.
Includes index.
1. Pacifism.   2. Just war doctrine.   I. Title.
JX1952.C26   1989   327.1′72   88-29547
ISBN 0-87722-603-2

For Sandy, Annie, and Ton

CONTENTS

Contents

PREFACE

As it happens with our children, so it does with our theories: they tend to become largely independent of their parents. And as it may happen with our children, so with our theories: we may gain from them a greater amount of knowledge than we originally imparted to them.

—Karl R. Popper,
Objective Knowledge

I have been haunted for the past several years by an idea that will not let me rest until it is written, however tentatively. This is as much a warning to the reader as a confession that I suspect I am onto something that may be beyond my capacities as writer and thinker. I am not apologizing for what follows; rather, I am trying to be frank. I invite the reader to join me in a struggle to understand a set of convictions at once admired for moral purity, strength, and idealism but all the while ridiculed as unrealistic, romantic, and fanatical: I am driven to attempt making theoretical sense of pacifism.

Pacifism rarely gets taken seriously. Academics and non-academics alike, when not ignoring it, seem to accept or (much more often) to reject pacifism in stereotyped extreme form. In our era the means of war make possible unimaginable destruction of whole nations, cultures, even our species and perhaps life itself. Yet pacifist alternatives to war are flippantly rejected as naive and misguided. Sadly, at the same time war is taken for granted as an unfortunate but necessary element of modern life. This is understandable. I was raised in the U.S. midwest in the 1950s, where conflict on any scale meant good guys and bad guys, my family, my school, my community, my state or country indelibly the former. It took the U.S. military involvement in southeast Asia for me to imagine pacifism as anything other than a misguided and fanatical illusion of the hopelessly naive; it has taken increasing awareness of the genuine prospect of thermonuclear war, looming persistently, to erode my academic sleepwalking and risk these thoughts about relations between values on war and peace.

My readers should know that I am a pacifist. But before too many hasty conclusions are drawn, let me add that I am a reluctant pacifist, never having imagined I might back into pacifism. The truth is, my reading, reflecting, and writing on the subject have drawn me into pacifism. Pacifism snuck up on me. There was no conversion experience such as popular stereotypes might lead one to expect. In fact I resisted the pull of pacifism because I feared being drawn to a moral extreme that I could not defend intellectually. Yet I came to realize that I could not intellectually defend dominant notions of just-war theory either. So I began trying to sort out what I could reasonably defend concerning the morality of peace and war. In the process I discovered a spectrum of views on the morality of war and peace and I have found myself within the pacifist segment. My perspective is that of a pacifist, but a peculiar sort of pacifist: one who has considered a range of positions on the ethics of peace and war and who has drifted from within the just-war segment of the continuum into the pacifist segment of the range. In fact I find myself at different points along the continuum depending on the wars and the means of war I am considering morally. I do not believe this is contradictory or that it results from indecision but from the subtlety, complexity, and difficulty of the factors relevant to moral judgment concerning war.

This book is a result of my struggle with a moral continuum. As such, it is for the most part theoretical and philosophical; it is to a small degree historical, but it is not at all theological. This emphasis is not out of hostility to theology or religion or to the views on pacifism and just war that various religious and theological traditions maintain. In fact, much of what I develop below is compatible with those traditions; but it is not grounded in theological convictions. Rather, my emphasis has been on values independent of religious conviction, values discovered and defended by reason and experience, values that are not necessarily derived only from religious faith but that may have secular grounds. This emphasis is a function of my interests and training. I leave to others the discussion of values anchored in religious or theological faith, and I leave open whether the values I find by my route may be identical to those that others find by theirs.

The book aims at a broad overview of the morality of peace and war and at the development and defense of a framework for understanding the spectrum of views. It opens with an examination of an important feature of modern Western culture. This reveals a pervasive, subconscious *warism*—an uncritical presumption in modern society that war is morally justifiable, even morally required. The war system, a standard operating procedure of modern nations constantly preparing for, threatening, and employing military force in domestic and international affairs, is largely taken for granted in contemporary society and goes almost wholly unquestioned within modern nations. In contrast we find pacifism frequently respected for moral strength yet widely considered to be an impossible ideal. The contrast between the idealistic values of traditional pacifism and the warism more realistically valued provides the context for the aims of this book: (1) to confront and expose the unconscious modern disposition to warism, (2) to correct the misconceptions that produce the popular stereotypes of pacifism, (3) to propose understanding the morality of peace and war by recognizing a value continuum that embraces a wide range of ethical positions between absolute pacifism on the one extreme and the so-called war "realism" at the other (the view that morality simply does not apply to war, that war happens outside of ethics, that there is no right or wrong about war, that morality is restored after war is over), (4) to consider a variety of reasons presented for and against various positions on the morality of war and (5) to entertain a range of views on a positive concept of peace as distinct from a concept of peace as the mere absence of war. Beyond these, I will defend my own inclination to settle between the extremes but in the pacifist segment of the continuum.

While warism is the frequent presumption of the moral justifiability of war, just-warism is a more critically adopted set of views on the moral issues related to war. A just-war continuum is described by reference to the dominant principles of the just-war tradition. A variety of views are seen between war realism at one extreme and pragmatic pacifism at the other. After a discussion of the relationship between means and ends in ethical thought generally, this distinction is used to understand similarities and differences among varieties of just-warism and varieties of pacifism. All but the most extreme pacifisms are seen to reject a clean separation between means and ends while most varieties of just-warism require such a split.

I give particular attention to the development of a typology of pacifism, a range of views that constitutes one segment of the continuum just mentioned above. Varieties of pacifism are united by two general convictions: the moral opposition to war and the moral disposition toward societies orderly from within by cooperation rather than orderly from outside by domination. A range of pacifist views is developed first to show differing grounds for moral opposition to war. Varieties of pacifism from absolute pacifism through collectivist, fallibility, and technological pacifisms to nuclear and pragmatic pacifism are described and principles accounting for the differences between each are explained. Finally a second pacifist continuum is considered, this time built upon the concept of positive peace as distinct from anti-war. A pacifist conception of positive peace is offered and peacebuilding methods from discussion and arbitration through protest and non-cooperation to nonviolent intervention are described.

With the cultural bias toward warism exposed and the misconceptions of pacifism set aside as the range of just-warist and pacifist thought is developed, familiar theoretical and practical objections to pacifism are examined. While neither pacifism nor just-warism can resolve all of the problems each must face, the standard objections are not the conclusive refutations they are sometimes taken to be.

The study closes with a summary and concluding discussion of the implications of the expanded and corrected spectrum of value positions on the morality of war and peace. The ethical continua presented (just-war, anti-war, and positive peace formulations) acknowledge complexity, encourage dialogue rather than polarizing views, and allow for moral maturity along the range of value positions. Backing into pacifism gradually or even occasionally comes to be understood as a coherent, justifiable moral response to the subtlety and confusion of relevant considerations on the morality of war. The scheme presented helps account for the reluctance to be pulled either to absolute pacifism (by conversion) or to war realism (by cynicism).

The book closes with a brief general history of the idea of pacifism. This is because we do not learn much about pacifism or pacifists as we are educated in the modern West (unless we are among the tiny minority of people raised with pacifist values; I was not). Occasionally we read or hear passing references to prominent pacifists like Gandhi, Jane Addams, or Martin Luther King, Jr., but serious consideration of pacifist value principles is rare at any level of public or private education in the modern West, especially when compared to the attention paid to military history, war heroes, and the dominant notion that the best guarantees of peace are the preparation for and threat of war. The brief overview of the history of moral resistance to war illustrates the range of pacifist thought developed in the theoretical chapters of the book.

My hope in writing this book is to prompt people to take pacifism seriously by pointing to the *range* of legitimately pacifist views united by the common convictions that war by its very nature is morally wrong and that humans should create communities orderly from within rather than ordered by force from without. Acknowledging varieties of pacifism distinct due to varying reasons for rejecting war and due to varying degrees of commitment to nonviolence should open dialogue about the nature of peace by challenging the polarized "dove" versus "hawk" pigeonholes into which we often force one another. Understanding the theoretical closeness between varieties of pacifism and varieties of just-warism should reduce the temptation to exaggerate differences among those genuinely concerned with the morality of peace and war and foster communication among those no longer seen to be moral opposites. At this point in time, alternatives to war are desperately needed and the first step is getting over the inclination to believe that the only alternative is surrender.

I do not pretend to resolve all of the problems of war in this little book; in fact, I do not directly address questions concerning the causes of war, the contemporary international tensions, the role of war in the great social and political ideologies, and so on. Rather, I limit my focus to the nature of moral reactions to war and peace. While primarily theoretical and philosophical, this work is not written for the technical professional philosopher but for a literate laity from secondary students and undergraduates in ethics and political thought to anyone interested in social and political issues, values, or peace studies, that is, for a general audience. I hope my reader will forgive my conceptual leaps and gaps; better, I hope that you can fill and correct them. I will be satisfied with contributing to an on-going discussion of these issues. While I cannot expect to resolve the many problems, perhaps I can entice others to try.

This book had its beginning in a proposal for an independent study project included in an application for an NEH Summer Seminar. While I did participate in the seminar on Utopian Literature during the summer of 1983, the director, Mulford Q. Sibley, worked his group so hard on the primary topic that I made rather little progress on my independent research. Perhaps in the spirit of NEH seminars, I never got over my proposal. In early November of 1983 I presented a paper, "Backing into Pacifism," at a conference on Philosophy, Morality, and Public Nuclear Policy at the University of Dayton. The paper was based on the NEH seminar proposal; reactions at the conference and to a version of the paper published in *Philosophy and Social Criticism* 10, nos. 3–4 (Winter 1984) provoked this attempt to develop ideas that were only suggested in the earlier presentations. The central ideas in the chapter on the ends and means of peace (Chapter III) were presented at a conference of International Philosophers for the Prevention of Nuclear Omnicide at St. Louis University in April of 1986. The grounds for technological pacifism (part of Chapter IV) were presented at an International Forum on Science, Technology, and Peace sponsored by UNESCO, the WFSW, and the Soviet Academy of Science in Moscow in July, 1986. The chapter on warism (Chapter I) is an expanded development of materials presented at a national meeting of Concerned Philosophers for Peace, October 1987, in Dayton, Ohio.

I am grateful to many individuals for help and support in this work. While disagreeing with a number of my claims, Mulford Q. Sibley, Professor Emeritus of Political Science and American Studies at the University of Minnesota, currently Professor of Jurisprudence at the School of Law, Hamline University, has been a challenging critic, generous with his time and encouragement. Karen Warren of Macalester College and Tom Moody of California State University, San Bernardino, have been cheerful, energetic, and constructive in their many suggestions. Nancy Holland of Hamline University, and Huston Smith, formerly at Hamline, have read various parts of the manuscript, making a number of important corrections and suggestions as have Dick Fuller of Gustavus Adolphus College and Bill Gay of the University of North Carolina, Charlotte. C. R. Moyer of Hamline University read the entire manuscript, providing stylistic corrections as well as substantive encouragement. I needed and am grateful for both.

I also appreciate the help of many members of Concerned Philosophers for Peace. Their gatherings, formal and informal, have been a reliable source of constructive criticism and support. Particular thanks must go to Joe Kunkel of the University of Dayton, a CPP driving force. I have discussed many of these issues during the past fifteen years with my good friends Hugh Stephenson of Red Wing,

Minnesota, and George Jones, Jr., of College Park, Maryland. Their influence is more important than they know. Numerous conversations with several former and current students were invaluable in refining and clarifying many of my thoughts; one former student in particular, Juliet Raulli, believed in what I was doing well before I did. Thanks must go as well to Jane Cullen of Temple University Press, to her reviewers (anonymous to me) who offered invaluable advice beyond recommending publication, and to Doris Braendel for expert copy-editing.

My gratitude goes also to Hamline University for making available Bush Foundation Faculty Development funds to reduce my teaching load by one course, for a Hanna Summer Research Grant, which allowed me to forgo summer teaching to devote more time to writing, and for a full semester sabbatical leave to revise and complete the manuscript for this book. I am indebted to Kenneth Wilson, Principal of Westminster College, Oxford, England, for helping me to arrange relocation to his institution for the writing sabbatical, and to Glynn Phillips, philosopher at Westminster, for his timely encouragement.

My greatest debt is to my family, who put up with my writing, rewriting, and editing in my head as I drive, hike, daydream, camp, do yard work, and play catch with the kids. More importantly, they manage to keep me in touch with the world beyond the academy, and they provide the harmony that makes possible some sense of balance between taking myself too seriously or too lightly.

D. L. C.
St. Paul, Minnesota
Summer, 1988

From
Warism
to
Pacifism

A Moral Continuum

CHAPTER I

WARISM

When you are criticizing the philosophy of an epoch, do not chiefly direct your attention to those intellectual positions which its exponents feel it necessary explicitly to defend. There will be some fundamental assumptions which adherents of all the variant systems within the epoch unconsciously presuppose. Such assumptions appear so obvious that people do not know what they are assuming because no other way of putting things has ever occurred to them.

—Alfred North Whitehead,
Science and the Modern World

Warism is the view that war is both morally justifiable in principle and often morally justified in fact. While this general view can be expressed in a variety of forms, the basic notion is that war can be morally acceptable and thus that alternatives to war may be entertained only insofar as they promise distinct advantages over war options. Pacifism, on the other hand, is the view that war, by its very nature, is morally wrong and that humans should work for peaceful resolution of conflict. This general view also can be expressed in a variety of forms; here the basic notion is that war is immoral and thus that alternatives to war must be discovered or created and practiced.

Pacifism rarely gets taken seriously in Western culture. Of course there are significant numbers of people who consider themselves to be pacifists, but they are a small minority of citizens in modern nations. The overwhelmingly dominant attitude in the history of Western thought has been to regard pacifism as a well-meaning but naive and misguided outlook; warism—the view that war is morally justifiable—is almost universally accepted. Warism is a primary cultural obstacle to taking pacifism seriously.

In every culture there are fundamental concepts, assumptions, ideas, and values that together form a frame of reference, a conceptual outlook, a world-view or perspective through which members of the culture experience the world. These fundamentals seem so obvious from within that it rarely occurs to members of a given culture that many of the most important ideas of their society are based on foundations that are taken for granted. One example in the Western tradition is the shift in perspective now called the Copernican Revolution. While the way the solar system works did not change, the perception of the workings of the solar system did change as we moved from an earth-centered model of the relationship between sun and planets to a sun-centered model. This change in basic outlook shook dominant institutions to their foundations. Since we now take the Copernican model for granted, it is hard for us to imagine the basic conceptual shift involved.

4

An example of a fundamental shift in perspective closer to our own experience can be seen in the ongoing reactions to the theory of evolution. People touched by Western science struggle to imagine the human species as emergent from less complex life forms. They do so within the context of traditional views of a divine creation of the human species. Some see the two models as compatible, but others see diametric opposition. Where the models are understood each to exclude the other, fundamental differences in perspective are at stake; one's entire orientation to reality—even to the meaning of life—may hinge on the difference between a divine source and a natural biological source of the human species. Questioning someone's perspective on such an issue can be threatening, not only because of the importance of the viewpoint but also because it may be a "given" to that individual.

Further examples of dominant societal conceptions can be seen in the significance of gender and race in determining economic, social, and educational opportunities in traditional Western culture. Without malicious intent people have taken for granted that women interested in medicine become nurses while men with those interests become doctors; women become secretaries, men become lawyers; and so on.[1] Minority races have been presumed fit only for unskilled labor while whites (white males) aspire to the professions. Here it should be obvious that the unconscious presuppositions about reality can have profound implications for values as well as beliefs. The cultural givens can be like normative lenses through which "reality" is conceived. Only after these lenses are acknowledged and examined can resulting prejudices be exposed. Making explicit the fundamental concepts—the normative lenses—that form the foundation perspectives of a culture is doing philosophy. So is questioning these fundamentals. And so is imagining alternatives. The more basic the hidden concepts, the more difficult is the examination of them.

In contemporary Western culture, warism is a dominant outlook. There is no special burden of moral justification that must be born by the warist; actually, the greater burden of justification rests with anti-warists. This very fact qualifies warism as the sort of unconscious fundamental presupposition to which Whitehead refers in the quotation at the head of this chapter. It seems so obvious to most of us that war is morally justifiable that we do not realize that we are assuming it; no other way of understanding large-scale human conflict has genuinely occurred to us. As Iredell Jenkins observes, "We appear to act on the assumption that wars are ultimate and ineradicable features of reality, so there are only two things we can do about them: delay their occurrence and make sure we win them when they occur."[2] Jenkins goes on to note that in fact we take war to be such an essential feature of the nature of things that it even seems natural to try to prevent war by threatening it.

The Western inclination to take warism for granted is so pervasive as to form an unexpressed attitude that is manifest in virtually all aspects of the culture from the obvious cases of politics and the popular media to business, education, and even religion. There is no conspiracy needed here; advertising, television, public and parochial school curricula, all tend to reflect the dominant outlook, the fundamental attitudes of the culture. This predisposition pervades culture from popular heroes like Rambo, Dirty Harry, GI Joe, and the Transformers to more esoteric heroes; even the scholar is considered to be the survivor of an academic joust, embattled in verbal attack and rejoinder. The philosopher is a warrior fighting for truth, defending honor and principle, exchanging linguistic blows in a struggle to defeat rivals and win arguments.[3] Virtually across all levels of society we see fights for superiority whenever conflict arises.

The traditional importance of autonomy of the individual, of personal integrity, of rights to privacy, property, and freedom from governmental interference in the lives of individuals, of fighting for what one believes in against all odds—all of these are examples of fundamental Western values that are for the most part uncritically adopted. Warism is another, but it is less noticed, less often acknowledged than these others. In history and government classes students learn about our republic: born in revolution, expanded through numerous battles with native American Indians, solidified in civil war, internationally preeminent after two world wars, a superpower strong in defense of freedom. School curricula offer many opportunities to discuss battles, tactics, heroics, and military leadership; however, one must dig to find mention of advocates of nonviolence, pacifists, models of cooperative rather than domineering domestic and foreign policy. This emphasis should be expected, given the fundamental perspectives that have been taken for granted.

To complicate matters further, Western culture has a tradition of attempting value-free education, placing little emphasis on ethical or political questioning of current or past social policy. Teachers are expected to teach facts and skills; values are to be respected but left to parents, family, and the church. Increased awareness that all teaching is laden with hidden values has tended to make parents and school boards more inclined to restrict materials that are at all controversial, thus avoiding the introduction of values that might be at odds with those traditionally dominant. This tends to reinforce the momentum toward uniformity and underscore *status quo* values. Entrenched in tradition and forming the fundamental perspective by which all judgments are made, the basic conceptions and values of a culture are rarely made explicit and even more rarely questioned from within the culture. When questions are raised, they tend to be met with defensive reactions, thus further underscoring the *status quo* values.

As a dominant attitude, warism is not limited to views reflected in popular culture and documented by mass opinion polls. Warren Steinkraus observes that "the great bulk of philosophers who have spoken on the question of war have supported and defended it as an instrument of social change."[4] Most often academic philosophers defend and justify war not for itself but as a means to important ends sought and achieved such as peace or self-defense. Steinkraus goes on to describe professional philosophers' reactions to war, saying "studied aloofness—which invariably means tacit acceptance"—is the most common attitude, followed by "overt defense of a particular national policy." The next most common attitude is "reluctant and even hesitant justification" and the least common is "direct criticism with or without consideration of alternatives."[5] This sequence could be extrapolated to describe academics in general, not just philosophers.

Further indication that our common cultural disposition is to consider war as morally justifiable—even morally required—is the fact that pacifists are much more frequently called upon to justify their views than are those who would defend war as a legitimate activity of nations. It is presumed that the burden of proof rests on those individuals morally opposed to war and committed to alternative means of resolving conflict. This is because warism is a cultural given, a national presupposition in the modern West. This is not to say that Western nations are necessarily belligerent; rather, it is to say that the war system, the standard operating procedure of sovereign states constantly preparing for, threatening, and employing military force in domestic and international affairs, goes almost wholly unquestioned. Those at various positions within the political spectrum may disagree about the details of weapons acquisitions budgets, levels of military preparedness, troop deployment, positioning of foreign military bases, and so on, but the system itself is not thereby in question. Given this context, criticism of the war system is typically met with hostility. Political candidates, understanding the dominant attitudes, need to present themselves as "tougher" than the other candidates, need to be wary of being characterized as "soft on the enemy," "weak on defense," "indecisive" with adversaries, or reluctant to "stand firm." All of this contributes to encouraging the dominant attitude and belittling its opposition. The result is that alternatives to the war system—pacifist views in particular—are not seriously considered because "everybody knows" what patently implausible positions these alternatives must be. This conventional wisdom is confirmed through its own media and institutions.

The widespread, unquestioning acceptance of warism and the corresponding reluctance to consider pacifism as a legitimate option make it difficult to propose a genuine consideration of pacifist alternatives. Typically, either it does not occur to the warist to challenge the view that war is morally justified or the warist openly accepts warism. In either case, the conceptual framework of the culture, which takes warism for granted, goes unquestioned. If we assume (without realizing it) that war itself is morally justifiable, our moral considerations of war will be focused on whether a particular war is justified or whether particular acts within a given war are morally acceptable. These are important concerns, but addressing them does not get at the fundamental issue raised by the pacifist: the morality of war as such. In *Just and Unjust Wars* Michael Walzer explains that "war is always judged twice, first with reference to the reasons states have for fighting, secondly with reference to the means they adopt." [6] The pacifist suggestion is that there is a third judgment of war that must be made prior to the other two: might war, by its very nature, be unjust? This issue is considered by Walzer only as an afterthought in an appendix, where it is tossed off as naive. Perhaps Walzer should not be faulted for this omission, since he defines his task as describing the conventional morality of war and, as has been maintained above, the conventional morality does take warism for granted. To this extent Walzer is correct. And this is just the point: our warist conceptual frameworks—our warist normative lenses—blind us to the root question. The concern of pacifists is to expose the hidden warist bias and not merely describe cultural values. Pacifists seek to examine cultural values and recommend what they ought to be. This is why the pacifist insists on judging war in itself, a judgment more fundamental than the more limited assessments of the morality of a given war or the morality of specific acts within a particular war.

The slow but persistent rise in awareness of racial, ethnic, and gender oppression in our time and the beginning efforts of liberation from within the oppressed groups offer hope that even the most deeply held and least explicitly challenged predispositions of culture might be examined. Such examinations can lead to changes in the lives of the oppressed. Perhaps even those oppressed by warism will one day free themselves from accepting war as an inevitable condition of nature.

Two hundred years ago slavery was a common and well-established social institution in the United States. It had been an ordinary feature of many cultures dating to ancient and perhaps prehistoric times. Slavery was taken for granted as a natural condition for beings who were thought to be inferior to the dominant group. And slavery was considered an essential feature of our nation's economy. Within the past two centuries attitudes toward slavery have changed dramatically. With these fundamental shifts in normative lenses came fundamental shifts in the practice and legality of slavery. These changes have been as difficult as they have been dramatic, for former slaves, for former slaveholders, and for culture at large. While deep racial prejudices persist to this day, slavery is no longer tolerated in modern cultures. Slavery-like conditions of severe economic exploitation of labor have become embarrassments to dominant groups in part because slavery is universally condemned. The point is that the most central values of cultures—thought to be essential to the very survival of the society and allegedly grounded in the natural conditions of creation—*can* change in fundamental ways in relatively short periods of time with profound implications for individuals and societies. John Dewey beautifully links this point to the consideration of warism: "War is as much a social pattern [for us] as was the domestic slavery which the ancients thought to be immutable fact."[7]

The civil rights movement has helped us see that human worth is not determined by a racial hierarchy. Feminism has helped us realize again that dominant attitudes about people may well be values we choose rather than innate and determined features of human nature. It is historically true that men have been more actively violent and have received more training and encouragement in violence than have women.[8] Dominant attitudes of culture have explained this by reference to what is "natural" for males and "natural" for females. By questioning the traditional role models of men and women, all of us become more free to choose the selves we are to be; we need not be defined by hidden presumptions of gender roles.

Parallel to racial and gender liberation movements, pacifism questions taking warism for granted. Pacifists seek an examination of our unquestioned assumption of warism to expose it as racism and sexism have been examined and exposed. Just as opponents of racism and sexism consider the oppression of non-whites and women, respectively, to be wrong and thus to require fundamental changes in society, so opponents of warism—pacifists of various sorts—consider war to be wrong and thus to require fundamental changes in society.

Related to the hidden presupposition of warism is a second cultural obstacle to taking pacifism seriously: pacifism is regularly confused with passivism. "Pacifism" (from the Latin *pax, pacis*, peace, originally a compact + *facere*, to make) means, simply, peacemaking or agreement-making. "Passivism" (from the Latin *passivus*, suffering) means being inert or inactive, suffering acceptance.[9] Pacifists may in fact be passivists but they need not be and indeed often are not. Pacifist activists are committed to making peace, making compacts by consensual agreement, contributing to harmonious co-operative social conduct that is orderly by itself from within rather than ordered by the imposition of coercion from without. There is more to pacifism than the moral opposition to war; there is the active effort to understand and make peace. As long as working for cooperative social conduct based on agreement without violence is confused with appeasement and suffering acceptance, there will be no viable alternatives to imposed and coercive social ordering. This confusion of pacifism with passivism accounts for the sometimes hysterical reactions with which pacifists are met when they make their pacifism known. Somehow pacifism has come to mean "giving up, giving in, selling out," descriptions more befitting passivists than pacifists. The truth is that pacifists typically reject passivism. Even Gandhi, the world's symbol of pacifism in the twentieth century, goes so far as to say that where the only choice is between violence and giving in, he would advise violence. Of course he goes on to say that the choice is virtually never so clear, that nonviolent options once sought can be found. Nevertheless, he states explicitly that pacifism "does not mean meek submission to the will of the evil-doer, but it means pitting one's whole soul against the will of the tyrant."[10] Pacifism is not passivism.

There is less confusion about the meaning of "war." According to its most famous characterization, war is "an act of violence to compel our enemy to do our will" and "there is no logical limit to the application of that force." "War is merely the continuation of policy by other means," composed of primordial violence, hatred, and enmity, the play of chance and reason.[11] In our era, unlimited, primordial violence is called "thermonuclear exchange," and when we think of war we think of tactical and strategic nuclear weapons. Etymologically, "war" (from Old High German *werra*, broil, confusion, strife) means, simply, discord.[12] War has come to mean hostile contention between groups by means of armed force. It is ironic that, culturally, we have lost sight of the positive meaning of peace—that is, concord, harmony—and think of peace as merely the absence of war. Yet it is war—that is, discord, dissonance, hostile contention between groups—that is the negative idea, a breach of agreement, a lack of cooperation, an absence of unity or harmony.

Beyond both cultural predisposition to warism and confusion of pacifism with passivism, a third obstacle to taking pacifism seriously is the widespread inclination to regard anyone sympathetic to peaceful alternatives to war to be a pacifist of the most extreme sort. The common conception is of pacifism as a monolithic, absolutist, religious or mystical conviction—usually arrived at by a conversion experience—that it is wrong always, everywhere, for anyone to use force against another human being. While this absolute position is one version of pacifism, it is not the only one, and it certainly is not the most commonly held version. Characterizing—better, caricaturing—all pacifists as holders of this doctrine polarizes discussion, creates confusion, and provokes defensive reactions. The result is pacifists' being called upon to defend the absolute view when their commitment is to pacifism of another sort. This misconception accounts for the frequent rhetorical question leveled at a pacifist: "You mean I don't have the right to defend myself against an unprovoked attack by a thug in a dark alley?!" (expressed with shock and disbelief). Very often this is raised not as a genuine question but in an effort to attack pacifism, to reduce it to what is popularly thought to be an absurd extreme. This is also attempted by asking, "Don't you believe in a police force?!" (said with a certain horror in the voice), and so on. Once it is recognized that there are several legitimate yet distinct versions of pacifism, then, as is argued below, the flippant dismissal or neglect of all moral opposition to war is exposed as superficial and confused.

The inclination to caricature pacifism as a dogmatic moral fanaticism is not limited to popular conventional wisdom. Pacifism is stereotyped in its most extreme form—what I have called absolute pacifism—and subsequently ridiculed by academics as well. Perhaps the most widely read and discussed philosophic consideration of pacifism since World War II is Jan Narveson's essay, "Pacifism: A Philosophical Analysis." [13] Briefly, Narveson tries to show that pacifism is "not merely radical" but "actually incoherent because self-contradictory." [14] He argues that the pacifist is in fact a hypocrite because while claiming to be completely opposed to violence the pacifist "is not willing to lift a finger to keep it from going on" except, perhaps, by handing out leaflets. [15] Clearly Narveson not only confuses pacifism with passivism but also presumes that violence is necessary to oppose violence. While carrying his caricature of the pacifist to this extreme, Narveson does not seem to realize that his own view, that is, that people have the right to do "whatever may be necessary" to defend themselves, may flirt with the morally opposite extreme (and thus the symmetrical contradiction): maybe an individual (or a village, or a nation) will have to be destroyed to be saved. As Cheyney Ryan puts it in his critique of Narveson, "It is not *obviously* permissible to torture another so as not to be tortured or to rain nuclear holocaust on another country to prevent such a fate for oneself." [16] At any rate, it seems fair to say that when it is not ignored by academics (which is the more usual treatment) pacifism can get caricatured and then dismissed on the basis of the distortion.

When the dominant attitudes of a culture are predisposed toward some ideas and against others, defending those widely embraced and rejecting those widely discounted is great sport. Dewey opens *Human Nature and Conduct* by drawing the reader's attention to just this point when he writes, "Give a dog a bad name and hang him." [17] That is to say, people and ideas can be dismissed readily when they do not have to be taken seriously because they are widely regarded as deserving dismissal. If the reputation is bad enough, the hanging is easy. If the reputation is a function of a distortive caricature and an unfriendly climate, it is too easy.

These cultural obstacles—the predisposition to warism, the confusion of pacifism with passivism, and the popular caricature of pacifism as a mystical moral fanaticism, unrealistic and naive—all contribute to and help create the hostile context in which pacifism is usually discussed. They come together in a dominant attitude: a good many people take "keeping the peace" to mean preserving the *status quo.* Those holding this concept of peace often enjoy an advantageous position within the *status quo,* that is, they see themselves as well-off in comparison with the social, economic, political, environmental, educational, and physical health of their peers, friends and neighbors, near and distant fellow humans. Any threat to the *status quo,* to the relative advantage, is often seen to require "defense against aggression," often without considering the possibility that the favored status itself may have oppressive implications for others. When some humans enjoy disproportionate advantage, others are subject to disproportionate disadvantage. This is not to suggest that justice requires an egalitarian distribution of benefits and burdens nor is it to deny it. Rather, the suggestion is that the pervasive view of keeping the peace as preserving current conditions, the notion that any threat to the way things are, any change, might "justify" the use of violence, is rooted in deeply entrenched assumptions about peace, war, and the *status quo*. These assumptions are challenged by pacifism. It is not surprising that those who regard peace to be the preservation of the *status quo* are inclined to regard peace advocates with suspicion. Pacifists threaten the *status quo*, especially the pervasive presumption of warism with its implications for the political and economic activities of a society. Emotional, intellectual, and moral strength are especially threatening to those used to dealing in physical strength. It should be no surprise that those who consider peace to be the preservation of the *status quo* are inclined to regard pacifism as incompatible with "the national security" and so on. Perhaps it is natural to see things from one's narrow interest perspective. It is easy to forget that America's eighteenth-century freedom fighters were terrorist guerillas to King George III.

All of these obstacles contribute to caricaturing and stereotyping rather than understanding pacifism. Certainly the same could be said, symmetrically, from the perspective of those in a disadvantaged status. They too might think of peace as the *status quo* and consequently reject pacifism, since preserving *that* sort of peace would be to perpetuate their own disadvantage. Even those seeing themselves to be in a middle position, neither advantaged nor disadvantaged within the *status quo*, might understand peace to be whatever current conditions are; the *status quo* is the familiar, something that can be counted on to a degree. Change, on the other hand, can be threatening because it promises the unfamiliar. And those somewhat discontent may take comfort in the relative stability of the *status quo* while fearing the unknown future circumstances that change would bring—maybe things would get worse rather than better. All this leads to the conclusion that social inertia favors conservatism unless conditions become extreme. Again, cultural obstacles preclude taking pacifism seriously.

No doubt there are many conditions that hinder the serious consideration of pacifism as a legitimate alternative to warism, conditions beyond the cultural presumption to warism, the inclination to dismiss peace theorists and activists as moral extremists, the confusion of pacifism with passivism, the disposition to regard alternatives to war as naive and unrealistic, and the notion that peace is preservation of the *status quo*. Surely one of these is the widespread view that, regardless of its moral merit, pacifism simply would not work. A host of objections to pacifism are variations on this theme: "It only works against *civilized* people like the British (Gandhi's struggle for Indian home rule) and the Americans (Martin Luther King's struggle for racial equality), but not all oppressive situations involve civilized people in positions of authority"; "What about Hitler?"; "Pacifism with the Communists? Be serious! They don't understand anything but military force"; "If everyone were a pacifist, then maybe it would work, but people just aren't." Another condition that hinders taking pacifism seriously is the frequent attitude that pacifists are well-meaning, kind, often courageous and sincere, yet self-righteous and abysmally naive. Sometimes pacifists are regarded as "copping out" to avoid the dirty-hands responsibilities of the real world. While these and other frequent objections to pacifism will be considered in what follows, the point in raising them here is to establish the prejudicial climate in which any consideration of pacifism must take place. Again, it is not just popular opinion that embodies these preconceptions; academics making the effort to address these issues often reflect the same negative dispositions, though they do so subtly and articulately.[18]

None of us can set aside all our preconceptions at will. But calling the possibility of their being prejudicial to our attention can make us wary and can help us to open our minds, to suspend disbelief, to listen and try to fathom how anyone could take pacifism seriously. It is not easy to make the effort to understand something that is at once respected for its moral strength and disregarded as utopian fantasy. Honesty and fairness demand a suspension of disbelief while recognizing the difficulty of the demand. As Karl Popper says, theoretical progress is made by a sympathetic grasp of the theory in question followed by the rigorous attempt to refute it. "There is no point in discussing or criticizing a theory unless we try all the time to put it in its strongest form, and to argue against it only in that form."[19] There will be no progress at taking peace seriously until the prevailing cultural dispositions to warism—academic as well as popular— are examined and exposed.

While philosophy is especially well suited to the task of examining and exposing warism and other cultural obstacles to understanding pacifism and peace, this is no easy undertaking. Plato opens Book VII of the *Republic* with the allegory of the cave, a warning to theorists who tamper with important cultural beliefs. Plato describes first the difficulty of letting go of our own attachments to our culture's dominant beliefs about reality. Later he tells of the anguish of the questioner turned teacher who tries to show others that they are caught in a spell of misconception taking dominant beliefs to be immutable features of nature. To develop minds with the courage and strength to question the most fundamental beliefs of culture is itself a difficult, dangerous business. Such minds threaten the *status quo* and are not well received; witness the scorn of those returning to the cave to challenge the basic beliefs of the cave dwellers. But philosophy cannot let dominant notions of culture go unquestioned, despite Plato's warning. Our task in the present context is to set aside the obstacles to taking pacifism seriously and to give sympathetic consideration to various formulations of pacifism. Only then have we put first things first, holding our objections until we have seen the position in its best light. When entertained in this spirit, pacifism is an interesting, challenging, and credible outlook.

Before going further we must recall that pacifism involves two general convictions, each of which gets expressed in a variety of forms by various pacifists. Pacifism is moral opposition to war *per se* and pacifism is commitment to cooperative social conduct based on agreement. As I understand the view, all pacifists will hold both of these convictions. But like any collection of individuals with common general principles, pacifists often disagree. They may have differing views about the grounds for accepting the two main principles, about the range of interpretations allowed within pacifism, about the limits beyond which one cannot go without leaving pacifism for warism, about the precise character of peace and the conditions required to foster it, about the relationships between means and ends in moral judgments of war, about the crucial reasons for rejecting war. While recognizing the complexity this diversity within unity poses, especially for those trying to sort out and understand the view, pacifists agree nonetheless on basic matters. Like any general view—social, political, religious, economic, aesthetic, even scientific—there may be diversity of opinion within general agreement. Consider the controversy within any political party or religious denomination about what constitutes a true adherent. Or think about the disagreements over whether rock is genuine music, whether free verse is real poetry, whether spilled paint can be art, even whether civil disobedience is patriotic behavior or whether a flat electroencephalogram signifies death. While it is important to recognize the essential nature of a general view, it is equally important to understand the diverse instances that it embraces.

In what follows, a range of moral positions on peace and war is described along with the reasons that account for their differences. Since most statements of pacifism begin with critiques of various justifications of war, we turn first to the just-war tradition to understand the principles and distinctions that have been used to provide moral justification for going to war and for various acts within war.

CHAPTER II

A JUST-WAR CONTINUUM

One of the things most of us want, even in war, is to act or to seem to act morally.

—Michael Walzer,
Just and Unjust Wars

The old adage, "all's fair in love and war," exposes a value position on war that goes back as far as human reflection. This is the view that war brings with it a suspension of moral judgment, that war happens outside the moral order. This view about war is called "realism." According to the war realist, war cannot be called right or wrong in any meaningful way; war is simply a fact. It is neither good nor evil but a fundamental state of nature where survival itself is at stake and where people do what they must to save themselves.

After a war is over, moral order is reestablished. But war itself is not an appropriate object of moral consideration.

The war-realist position has had distinguished and articulate exponents since ancient times.[1] But parallel to the explicit defense of war realism there has been a vast and equally long tradition of moralizing about war, of claiming various wars to be more or less justified, of claiming specific acts within wars to be more or less warranted. Nations and leaders have throughout history claimed to be in the right concerning their participation in war, and their critics have challenged their claims.

Warism—the view that war is both morally justifiable in principle and often morally justified in fact—stands in an interesting relationship to war realism. While the war realist claims that war is not an appropriate object of moral consideration, this can in fact be taken as a kind of justification of war: war is exempt from moral condemnation and thus is to be expected as a natural condition of human society. An ironic and tacit justification emerges from the very claim that war is outside the moral order. In this way it can be said that war realism is the most extreme form of warism. When war realism is taken for granted, all moral questions concerning war are dismissed as naive and confused. War must be accepted as a fact of nature.

Sometimes war realists claim that the realist view results from the logic of war itself. According to Carl von Clausewitz, "War is an act of force which theoretically can have no limits."[2] Clausewitz goes so far as to say that introducing restraint to war is committing absurdity because war naturally involves adversaries forcing one another to continuous, reciprocal escalation. To him, the only limits to war would be the limits of the means of war.[3] Thus the introduction of any *moral* restraint in war, on this understanding of the logic of war, would be the cessation of genuine war. According to the war realist, then, all war becomes total war. The only limits to war are the suspension of war through victory or surrender and the inherent limits of the means of particular wars, limits of technical, economic, or practical necessity.

Although war realism is the extreme limit of warism, there is a wide range of warism that rejects realism. We will call this range of views on the morality of war "just-warism." Perhaps an appropriate beginning to a discussion of just-warism would be an account of *why* war realism is rejected. On what basis can we moralize about war, or about anything else for that matter? This question opens a floodgate of issues that cannot be ignored but cannot be adequately resolved all at once.

The general question of the foundation or source of values by which we make moral judgments is widely disputed. There are competing answers to the search for these foundations (including a rejection of the need for foundations); a variety of positions will be considered throughout this study. The most important evidence against war realism is the fact that people for centuries have believed that war *is* an appropriate object of moral judgment. Moral justifications for wars and acts of war have been made, presumably because such actions needed to be justified within their cultural contexts. In what follows we will examine this tradition of the moral consideration of war in order to expose and understand the principles by which such moral discourse has meaning. By appealing to tradition we do not focus on what people have done—their behavior—but on what they thought they ought to have done, that is, on their values, their aspirations, their ideals.

It is important to understand that just-warism is not a precise and explicit doctrine of any government, international body, treaty, church, or moral theory. Rather, just-warism is a tradition, a generally accepted if variously interpreted set of guidelines about morality and war that has been evolving in Western society throughout history. It involves broadly cultural values in addition to more narrowly religious, military, and professional elements. Moral judgments of war can be found in ancient literature and philosophy as well as in medieval theology, modern history, and contemporary military codes of conduct.

Broadly speaking, the just-war tradition consists of two distinct but interrelated themes: the moral justification for going to war and the moral limits of fighting a war. The first is called the *jus ad bellum.* It consists of principles that offer guidance on when a resort to war is justified. The second theme, the *jus in bello,* offers principles that outline the moral limits or restraint required in the fighting of a just war. After a general characterization of the principles of each aspect of just war, the necessary conditions will be described in greater detail, concluding with a consideration of the implications of the tradition in outlining a range of just-warist positions.[4]

The *jus ad bellum,* the moral justification for resorting to war, requires that six distinct conditions be met: (1) the proposed war must be fought for a *just cause,* (2) the decision to go to war must be made by *right authority,* (3) nations entering war must do so with *right intention,* (4) war must be an act of *last resort,* (5) the prospect for an *emergent peace* must be, more likely than not, the result of the war, and (6) the total evil of the acts of war to be undertaken must be *proportionate* to the good achieved (that is, the total evil of a just war may not exceed the good to be gained). Each of these conditions must be considered independently before conclusions can be drawn about the *jus ad bellum* portion of the just-war tradition.

Within the Western value heritage, a war has been thought to be undertaken for a *just cause* if the war is in response to particular aggressive actions. As Walzer puts it, the just-war tradition maintains that "it is a crime to commit aggression" and "it is right to resist aggression."[5] The context for understanding what counts as aggression includes a system of independent states, each having discrete territorial integrity and political sovereignty. Any use or threat of force by one state against the political sovereignty or territorial integrity of another constitutes aggression. Thus every just war is undertaken in response to a wrong committed. A just cause may be self-defense, because a state's own territory is threatened by force, or it may be the defense of another sovereign state threatened by aggression. While the just cause has been for the most part limited to states fighting for political sovereignty and territorial integrity, the principle has evolved to include acts to balance intervention of other states, to rescue or protect potential victims of massacre, to assist secessionists, and even to strike preemptively against potential threats. Clearly the principle of *just cause* has both a firm moral footing and an elastic boundary. Like any moral principle, it can be abused, rationalized, and manipulated by propaganda; national leaders may accuse others of aggression or insist that their own actions are defensive when in fact they are acting to protect vested interests independent of moral considerations. And states can quite genuinely believe themselves to be acting for a just cause when their own biases may distort their moral reasoning. But recognizing difficulties in specific applications of the principle does not dismiss it as an important element of the just-war tradition.

A morally justified decision to go to war must not only meet requirements for a just cause but must also be made by *right authority*. Historically, "right authority" means the legitimized decision makers of government. Heads of state, rulers, governors claim to be or are charged with acting in behalf of their citizens. Monarchs, presidents, and prime ministers act by virtue of their offices; legislative bodies make formal declarations of war deliberating as representatives of the people. Within the past few hundred years the principle of right authority has shifted from resting with single individuals—for example, an autocratic monarch's claim to power—toward resting with the collective will of those people directly affected by the threats, potential gains, and burdens of war. Wars of revolution are justified by appeal to rights of various sorts and by appeal to defense against exploitation, aggression, and denial of participation in government. As was seen with the requirement of just cause, right authority, the second principle required for justly going to war also is open to abuse and rationalization. There can be illegitimate claims to right authority. Yet the moral strength of the principle rests on a firm value tradition of expecting decisions of nations to be non-arbitrary and systematically grounded, anchored within the society, that is, to be legitimate. Certainly the decision to take a nation to war must rest with legitimate authority.

The third requisite for *jus ad bellum* is *right intention*. Wrong intention is "the desire for harming, the cruelty of avenging, an unruly and implacable animosity, the rage of rebellion, the lust of domination and the like."[6] Right intention wills acts to right a wrong and bring about peace in place of conflict. Of course this is a psychological element of just war. Who can know the intention of another? Who can be certain even of their own intent? Yet intention can be measured to some degree by actions. Excessive force, overkill, humiliating domination, and the persistent preparation for these, all indicate the likely absence of right intention.

Fourth, any just war must be undertaken only as a *last resort,* only when all other avenues for righting the wrongs threatened or enacted have been exhausted. The presumption of the just-war tradition is that war is morally abhorrent and must be avoided if at all possible. The burden of proof does not rest on those trying to avoid war; the justificatory burden rests squarely on those who propose to go to war. As with the other principles above, there are varying interpretations of what constitutes last resort. Just-warist James Turner Johnson goes so far as to say that "whatever contemporary international law may say or be interpreted to say, the weight of Western moral tradition on war does not rule out that in some cases first use of force may appropriately be a response of last resort."[7] Clearly, "last resort" can be stretched to cover a wide range of actions.

The likelihood that *peace will emerge* as a consequence of entering into war is a fifth condition for a moral justification to go to war. War cannot be justly undertaken unless it is more likely than not to generate conditions of lasting peace, conditions that set right the problems that provoked the acts of aggression that triggered the war. This principle too is open to broad interpretation. Whether the imposition of will by force can provide a likely basis for lasting peace is a debatable issue. The extent to which peace rests on co-operative rather than forced and coercive activity will figure into the debate. In any event, the genuine prospects for resolving the problems that produced the breach of peace are to be considered in the moral justification of going to war.

Finally, the *jus ad bellum* requires that the total evil resulting from going to war cannot exceed the total good to be achieved by war. This is the principle of *proportionality*. It is an important element in both the *jus ad bellum* and *jus in bello* sides of the just-war tradition. Here, the point is to consider the total scope of the war that is about to commence. If the price of the war is too high in terms of total costs to the people in whose name it is fought—the costs in total dislocation and suffering as well as in economic and human sacrifice—then the war cannot be justified morally. The evil may not be disproportionate, may not exceed the good attained. This is an especially difficult factor to consider because it is so speculative in character. Certainly there are varying interpretations of this principle as it is invoked concerning any particular war.

Considering whether it is just to go to war from within the value principles of the just-warist tradition is a complex and difficult set of tasks. Perhaps the most difficult feature of the determination is in holding the six principles in mind, keeping them together, and achieving the confident conclusion that all six factors have been judiciously weighed and that the war in question qualifies as one that it would be just to undertake. Certainly each of the six principles is open to a range of interpretations. Beyond this, the principles get different emphases as parts of the set of requirements for *jus ad bellum*. Wars are sometimes called just on the strength of their satisfying or seeming to satisfy one or more of the principles. The social and psychological factors involved in generating popular support for a given war may distort or cloud individual and collective judgments either for or against the moral justifiability of going to war. War fever—or anti-war fever—can skew the weighing of morally relevant factors. All of this means that, while there is a generally accepted traditional set of guidelines for determining the moral justifiability of going to war, there is no guarantee that the guidelines will produce consistent and predictable results. Many factors *beyond* the morally relevant ones enter into the social determination: historical animosities, fortunes to be made or lost, racial, ethnic, religious, and cultural prejudices and fears, treaties, alliances, old friendships, historical partnerships, and so on. Clearly, deciding that a given war is one justly entered is a complex, subtle, and confusing process. Even the most honest, fair, sincere, and thorough considerations may not yield identical conclusions about a given war.

Setting aside the complexity and difficulty of the *jus ad bellum* for the moment, assuming that the conditions are met to a fairly strong degree of consensus among those bearing the risks and burdens of war, in addition the just-war tradition demands *jus in bello*. That is, even if we grant that in a given case it is just to go to war, still we must go on to satisfy the principles of the tradition that guide us to assure that the war is justly fought. The just-war tradition rejects war realism, so not all is fair in war. The *jus in bello* provides principles to guide us concerning the moral restraint required for the just fighting of a war: discrimination and proportionality.

The *jus in bello* principle of *discrimination* means that, in just war, non-combatants are immune from attack. It is always wrong to kill innocents. The point is that those making war must *discriminate* between the war's participants and those caught in the crossfire. The notion of non-combatant immunity seems to have its source not in religious or moral sensitivity but in a code of chivalry from the Middle Ages. Knights were professional soldiers; "there was no glory in armed combat with a nonknight." Besides, "noncombatant serfs, peasants, artisans and merchants were the source of the wealth of members of the knightly class." It was cowardly to attack an enemy through his non-combatant subjects rather than directly, and knights had a vested interest in protecting and supporting the non-combatants who were the source of their own wealth.[8] The principle of non-combatant immunity has developed and persisted through the tradition.

While it seems obvious that children, the elderly, and other non-combatants are not appropriate targets of the means of war, the question of innocence is a difficult one. The relevant distinction, according to Walzer, "is not between those who work for the war effort and those who do not, but between those who make what soldiers need to fight and those who make what they need to live, like all the rest of us."[9] Thus, producers of food and clothing are innocents, but armament factory workers are not. Certainly there are differing degrees of active and direct involvement in the war effort. Those in the media or mail service, for instance, may be more or less directly contributing to an efficient war operation. But the existence of problematic cases does not mean that there are no clear cases. Surely children are innocents in war. As such, they are never targeted if the war is justly fought.

Even if the question of innocence could be resolved easily, still there is a related problem about non-combatant immunity. Can a military target be destroyed if the destruction may collaterally injure innocents? For example, can a strategic bridge or munitions factory be targeted and bombed if there may be injury or death to innocents who happen to be in the vicinity when the bombing takes place? In an effort to resolve problems like this for Christians committed to their moral tradition yet equally committed to their nations' war efforts, Catholic writers in the Middle Ages worked out the notion of the *double effect*.[10]

The thrust of the notion of double effect is that the injury or death of innocents, while always wrong, can be excused if certain conditions hold, namely, that the death or injury of innocents was not the intended effect of the act of war, that the direct or intended effect was itself justifiable, and that the good of achieving the intended effect outweighs the evil of the unintended, secondary, or collateral effect, the death or injury to innocents. Applied to the example above, the principle of double effect would allow the targeting and destruction of a strategic bridge or munitions plant within the framework of a justly fought war because the injuries and deaths of innocents who just happened to be victims of the bombing were not intended, the bombing of such legitimate targets of war was justified, and the innocent injuries and deaths, while regrettable, were outweighed by the good to be achieved through the destruction of military targets. The point is that acts of war can have double effects: those legitimate and intended and those in a sense accidental and unintended. The goal or first effect is distinguished from the by-products or second effect. Once again we have a principle of the just-war tradition that is open to a range of interpretations and that can be abused to rationalize the commission of great evils in war. One may argue, for example, that the nuclear bombing of Nagasaki in August of 1945 was intended to destroy legitimate military targets and only collaterally injured and killed thousands of innocents. But if the deaths and injuries of innocents were expected outcomes of the bombing, how could they be excused as unintended? While open to broad interpretation and abuse, the principle of double effect has a moral basis in just-warism and is necessary to explain the tradition's reluctance to reject all acts of war that unintentionally and incidentally involve victimization of innocents.

Closely related to the principle of double effect—so closely that it monitors the invocation of the principle—is the notion of proportionality. Above, proportionality was discussed as it figures into the *jus ad bellum* aspect of just-warism. There the concern was with the overall evils of the acts of war as balanced against the overall good to be achieved by war. Here, as a key feature of the justly fought war, proportionality is used to calculate the moral permissibility of specific acts of war. The question is always, "Does the good result expected outweigh the evil of the act proposed?" If the action is disproportionate—if it results in more evil than good—then the act is not permitted, even if the good is very important. So we have yet another somewhat slippery guideline that calls for speculation and is open to abuse and rationalization. Yet this principle too is crucial to the just-war tradition, crucial because it is the fundamental principle of moral restraint of the just-warist tradition and as such it is what distinguishes the just-warist from the war realist.

The war realist believes that war is outside of morality, that war is amoral. Consequently the war realist is committed to total war whenever war happens, because there is no moral restraint to war. To the war realist, wars must be won at any cost. The just-warist, in contrast, believes that war must be justified morally. And for the just-warist, it is possible to be faced with the awful dilemma of having to decide whether to surrender and lose a winnable war and hold to the principles of restraint from the moral tradition *or* to sacrifice the principles of moral restraint and win, even though such winning would be by unjust means. For the just-warist, if the costs of war in evil exceed the gains in good, the war cannot be justly undertaken. And if the fighting of the war cannot be done fairly, within the conditions of discrimination and proportionality honestly applied, then the war cannot be justified. At both levels, in total evil overall and in evil arising battle by battle, tactic by tactic, proportionality is the reigning principle that separates the just-war tradition from war realism. Even if a nation is justified in going to war, it must not do so if the war cannot be justly fought.

One of the most disturbing developments of the just-war tradition in the twentieth century has been the tendency away from moral restraint in war, the tendency toward total war. In World War I and in World War II "Western culture came to accept the rightness of un-limited means of war—the shelling of cities and gas warfare of World War I, and in World War II the obliteration of population centers by conventional explosives, napalm and finally atomic weapons." [11] This drift toward accepting total war runs counter to the just war tradition of regarding war as sometimes justifiable yet only practiced with restraint.[12] The post-World War II arms race with its weapons of unspeakable horror signals further the drift toward the war-realist position. Yet the just-warist tradition has not been abandoned. As evidence for this we can note the persistent need of politicians, military personnel, and ordinary citizens to justify or at least to seem to justify the war system on moral grounds.

Having reviewed the just-war tradition, we can pause, reflect, and take an overview perspective on the moral guidance the tradition provides. The moral strength of the tradition seems to rest in its persistent and generally accepted basic principles of fairness, restraint, and justice. Given the context of a diverse collection of nation states, the sovereignty and integrity of each is the valued commodity; only the breach of political sovereignty or territorial integrity provides moral justification for acts of war in response to aggression. Specific conditions restrain both an overeager and an overactive interest in participation in war. And other conditions restrain the means of war once war happens. Despite the weight of tradition and the common sense of the guidelines, there are dangers with the application of just-warist principles. The guides have unclear—even elastic—boundaries that can be interpreted in a range of ways leading to very different conclusions about the justifiability of wars and acts of war. And like any moral principles, these can be abused as well as used as vested interests cloud and distort even our most genuine and serious reflections.

As a result of the vagueness, variety, and elasticity of this set of principles, it is possible to sketch a range or spectrum of views within the just-warist tradition. Also as a result of the vagueness, variety, and elasticity of the tradition, it is not possible to describe this range with a high level of precision. Perhaps we should keep Aristotle's warning in mind that we should expect no more precision than a subject matter will allow. We can imagine a moral continuum within the just-war tradition, but we cannot draw clean and clear lines between positions nor can we hold given individuals to specific places along the scale.

At one extreme along the proposed continuum we find those who call themselves just-warists, who believe themselves to be within the tradition, but who are so ready to justify even totally unrestrained war as to place themselves on the periphery of just-warism alongside war realism. Those holding such views on the morality of war are very nearly as "hawkish" as the genuine war realist, not in eagerness to go to war but in willingness to accept war as an inevitable natural event.

We move away from the brink of war realism as we take moral restraint with increasing seriousness. The more thoroughly and carefully we consider the full set of *jus ad bellum* and *jus in bello* principles, the more meticulously we guard against rationalization and the prejudice of vested interest. The more judiciously we consider the perspectives of our adversaries as they weigh the rights and wrongs of alleged aggression, the more cautious we become at claiming justification for our entry into war and for our means of war.

The temptation is to suggest that the just-warist range of views leaves off where the pacifist range picks up, but this seems too quick and too simple. In fact there seems to be a good deal of overlap between the pacifist and the just-warist views. After all, pacifism like just-warism is committed to moral restraint in going to war and in fighting war. While the pacifist range of views is not developed until Chapters IV and V below, it can be said that not all pacifists are of the absolute sort, just as not all warists are war realists. There are degrees of moral opposition to war, degrees of commitment to the resolution of conflict without violence, degrees of interest in guaranteeing that war is a last resort, that peaceful alternatives to war are exhausted, degrees of confidence in the likelihood of and commitment to creating emergent peace. The telling distinction between pacifists and just-warists is whether they believe *both* that war is justifiable in principle *and* that war is justified in fact in a given case. As we will see below, there are varieties of pacifism where war is accepted as legitimate in principle but war is rejected as illegitimate in fact, because the means of war cannot meet the demands of the just-war tradition. Perhaps some of the confusion on these distinctions can be straightened out below as the pacifist continuum is developed. The point here is to note that pacifists and just-warists can and do share many of the same moral concerns. Pacifism and just-warism are *not* moral opposites but are differences of degree along a much wider value scale.

One of the most telling indicators of one's position along the just-warist segment of the proposed moral continuum is the level of confidence, the strength of knowledge, that is required for justifying war. Just-warists will vary in position along the scale in direct relation to the extent of knowledge and evidence they expect to verify compliance with each of the principles of the tradition. If they are quick and eager to justify entering a war and loose in demanding moral restraint on how it is fought, and if they have only a casual interest in the presentation of evidence to satisfy some of the guiding principles for just war, then they fall closer to the war-realist extreme at the periphery of just-warism. If, on the other hand, they have scrupulous demands that each principle be considered and if they have high expectations for the evidence satisfying each just-war principle, then they would fall further away from the war-realist extreme toward the weak end of the scale. This is why it is easier to justify a small-scale, clear-cut, "surgical" military action to rescue civilians from terrorist kidnappings than to justify a preemptive strike of nuclear weapons against a potential adversary. One can imagine a credibility scale whereby the smaller, closer, more direct and evident the aggression *and* the smaller, closer, more evident and manageable the response *and* the more likely its success, then the easier is the burden of justification. Distant, obscure, speculative military engagements undertaken at high risk with doubtful motives and questionable results are much more difficult to justify. One's place along the just-warist continuum seems to be a function of one's knowledge of the justifiability of proposed acts. This will vary from person to person both with differing standards and expectations as to what counts as justification *and* with more elusive, evasive, and speculative prospective wars for which the justificatory burden is simply greater. The more one must know and the better one must know it, the further one is from the war-realist extreme.

It should be clear, then, that there are two factors that determine one's place along the just-warist continuum: the sort of war under consideration and the standards of knowledge and evidence that must be met to satisfy the just-war-tradition principles. These are interrelated because the larger the scale of any given war, the more there is to know in order to weigh the various considerations. This issue of scale is why some of the more eager just-warists will justify acts of war by calling them "policing actions." The analogy shifts us from thinking on a large scale—armies and nations—to thinking on a small scale—police officers and criminals. Of course there are further problems with the analogy: true police actions are undertaken to *apprehend* criminals so they may face trial. True police officers do not punish nor do they decide guilt. In civilized societies it is *unusual* for police officers to have killed criminals.[13] But in acts of war dubbed "police actions," soldiers are supposed to kill; enemy soldiers are certainly not apprehended to face trial. The point is that the smaller-scale acts of war have greater likelihood of being justified because the relevant factors are more manageable. This is why scale-reducing analogies are used, to persuade (oneself and others) that a given act of war is morally acceptable. Beyond this, of course, is the second factor: the more demanding one is concerning standards of compliance with the guidelines for just war, the more difficult will be the moral justification of war, regardless of scale.

One result of our consideration of the just-warist tradition is that we have found that believing in just war is no simple matter. Further, we have seen that there is room for a wide range of positions within the just-warist tradition, from the brink of war realism on one extreme to considerable overlap with the weaker forms of pacifism on the other. Finally, we have seen that just-warist positions vary in degree both with the scale of the war in question and with the standards of evidence required to satisfy just-war conditions. If we think of the magnitude of war ranging from all-out thermonuclear exchange among all nuclear powers at one extreme through degrees of limited nuclear war (if such are possible) and degrees of conventional war down to the smallest-scale domestic uprisings and finally to responses to terrorist incidents at the small-scale extreme, it is clear that the burden of justification is more manageable toward the small-scale extreme.

Concerning the varying standards of evidence required for compliance with just-warist guidelines of restraint, attention must be paid to the considerable variation over emphasis or relative importance of the different principles. To a just-warist like James Turner Johnson, proportionality and restraint cannot be forsaken (although he hedges on this toward the end of *Can Modern War Be Just?*). To a just-warist like Michael Walzer, there are cases of "extreme emergency" where proportionality and restraint can be suspended out of necessity in order to guarantee the outcome of a particular war. As Walzer argues the point:

> A world where entire peoples are enslaved or massacred is literally unbearable. For the survival and freedom of political communities—whose members share a way of life developed by their ancestors, to be passed on to their children—are the highest values of international society. Nazism challenged these values on a grand scale, but challenges more narrowly conceived, if they are of the same kind, have similar moral consequences. They bring us under the rule of necessity (and necessity knows no rules).[14]

Walzer goes on to caution against too quickly overriding the rules of just war by appeal to the necessity prompted by supreme emergency, lest we slide into war realism. But clearly this opens the door, if only slightly, to any particular threat's being perceived or characterized to justify overriding the restraint of the just-warist tradition. So a cause may be so just as to require acts normally morally prohibited.

When we begin to talk about goals or ends of war so precious that they may warrant suspending the moral restraint in war ordinarily demanded by the just-warist tradition, we have encountered one of the most difficult problems facing any moral consideration of war, namely, the problem of weighing the ends in view against the means proposed to achieve them. The question of the relationship between the means and ends in the morality of war—in ethics generally—is one so difficult and crucial that it requires a thorough consideration in its own right. The next stage in understanding the moral continuum between war realism and absolute pacifism must be an examination of the means and ends of war and peace. Only after grappling with this problem can we go on to the pacifist segment of the continuum.

CHAPTER III

MEANS AND ENDS

Show us not the aim without the way.
For ends and means on earth are so entangled
That changing one you change the other too;
Each different path brings other ends in view.

—Ferdinand Lassalle,
Frans von Sickingen

War is never valued as good in itself; war has no intrinsic value. In fact, rarely is war considered good at all. Even when war is thought to be justified in certain circumstances, those justifying it do not claim that war is good but that it is a necessary evil or that it is acceptable as a means to some other end. While granting that acts of war generate suffering, destruction, death, dislocation, and other evils, the advocate of just war—the just-warist—argues that all of this can be outweighed or defeated by the ultimate good that can come from fighting the war. Of course such claims lose their credibility as the ends in view elude warmakers. Some just-warists might go so far as to say that a given war ought to be fought even though it is likely to be lost since it is somehow better to go down to defeat in the right than surrender to an unjust enemy. The point is that whenever war is accepted morally it is so not for itself but as a means to something else. This raises the very difficult issue of the relationship between means and ends in the ethics of war and peace.

While varieties of pacifism differ over grounds for moral opposition to war and over models of positive peace, all pacifists regard war as immoral by its nature and go beyond the just-warist to reject a means/ends justification of war. Before we can describe the range of pacifist thought, we must examine the debate between just-warists and pacifists on the means/ends issue.

Traditional ethics is the systematic study of principles of right action or correct behavior. Ethical theorists try to unify the various beliefs about right and wrong human activity in order to establish non-arbitrary and consistent foundations for morality. While there is a great deal of disagreement among ethical theorists, all ethical theories reject moral skepticism—the belief that no rational sense can be made of calling human behavior right or wrong—and set forth reasons for basic principles or criteria of moral behavior. Ethical theories differ with the kinds of reasons offered as grounds for moral claims.

The reasons we have for valuing what we do are themselves controversial. Ethical theorists do not all agree on the source, basis, or foundation for valuation. "Value" comes from the Latin word "valere" and means, simply, "to be of worth." Our values reflect what we hold to be of worth. Values differ within cultures as well as between cultures. There is no scholarly consensus about what we *ought* to value, and we cannot expect to settle this problem here in any final way. In recognizing this feature of our study we acknowledge the problem of first principles: on what basis can we begin to defend any values?

One way to settle this problem of first principles is to ground values in God. On such views, divine commands establish the basis for morality. The Judeo-Christian Ten Commandments are one example of a divine-command foundation for morality. But of course different religious traditions offer different basic principles also justified as divinely commanded. And even within one religious tradition there arise conflicting interpretations of the meanings and implications of the basic principles. Other ethical theories turn to moral intuition for a foundation. They argue that humans by nature have a more or less reliable intuitive sense about right and wrong. They disagree over the extent to which this moral intuition may be distorted or corrupted by cultural conditions, and they offer varying methods to test the authenticity of moral intuitions. Still other moral theorists see values to be grounded in historical, economic, and cultural conditions and see the so-called intuition to be a function of experience alone. Some hold that our values are so deeply embedded in our language that we embrace values unconsciously as we learn to function within a language. Recognizing the pervasive problems at the foundation of morality, moral theorists persist in looking for reasons to justify moral choices. Here, we have been working from within a loosely understood moral framework of values developed over more than 2,500 years into a tradition on morality and war, a moral framework influenced by all the perspectives on the foundation of morals just mentioned, a moral tradition evolving with the cultures it helped shape.

Traditional ethical thought can be divided broadly into two categories: first, theories that claim some acts to be morally obligatory regardless of their consequences (these are called "deontological" from the Greek *deon* [duty] + *logos* [rational account]) and second, theories that base the rightness of an action on its likely results (these are called "teleological" from the Greek *telos* [end, goal] + *logos*). This distinction between duty-based and consequence-based moral justifications for actions is often regarded as a fundamental polarity in ethical thought.[1]

When we consider the polar extremes on the means/ends spectrum in ordinary moral discourse ("results mean nothing" at one extreme, "results mean everything" at the other), we see that each is ridiculed on moral grounds by its polar opposite. Consider the familiar, "How can you say we can never tell a lie, even to save an innocent person's life?" (asked with genuine disbelief). Here the consequentialists remind those duty-bound of the high price of purism, suggesting, for example, that a lie to a terrorist is a trivial wrong compared to the good end to be achieved in saving an innocent life. On the other hand, consider the equally familiar, "What possible end could justify nuclear war?" (asked with similar disbelief). In this case the suggestion is that the means are too horrible to employ, no matter *how* good the cause at stake. In both cases the appeal is made to the polar opposite moral emphasis. These appeals, in various forms fitting the moral conflict at hand, do give us pause to reflect on the extremes to which we will go in acting on principles. They are credible enough to keep the debate between duty-based and results-based ethics going strong. They also help us realize that we often rationalize our moral dilemmas, appealing alternately to duty or consequences, depending on convenience. In our honest and genuine moral choices, most of us consider our obligations as well as the likely consequences of our possible actions; and most of us could not say precisely how and why we give the emphasis we do in various circumstances, more toward duty in some cases, more toward results in others.

The theoretical problem is the same for both extremes: how can we take the end into consideration without making it *the* justification for any and all means? Or, from the opposite perspective, how can we insist that we are duty-bound to an action without taking into consideration *any* aspects of the likely consequences of the act? We cannot pretend to provide a definitive resolution to this dilemma, but we can hope to make headway by calling into question the supposition that means and ends are cleanly separate. After all, our moral objectives are not independent, split off and separate from our decisions and activities. Rather than the achievement of certain isolated objectives, the moral life is a process of living, deciding, acting in ways compatible with and contributing to our vision of the good life. Being moral is not like winning a game where various means are manipulated toward one end. Perhaps, as Antony Flew argues, leading a moral life is not attempting or achieving ends or objectives at all. Ordinarily, when we think of being moral we think of keeping promises, paying debts, looking after dependents, being honest, generous, and kind, all the while avoiding cruelty, lying, stealing, and so on.[2] When we think of these as central to a moral life, it is not because they are mere means to some end or because they are required by some absolute principle(s) without consideration of their likely effects, but because they constitute the activity of a moral life, good in themselves, expressions of respect for kindred humans, as well as likely to be productive of good results. In our ordinary lives we do not regard means and ends as separate, independent, distinct from one another. In fact we work toward the integrated life, where our activities are compatible with and appropriate to our goals.

Beyond this, we need to recognize that even when the moral thing to do *is* to achieve certain consequences, those consequences are as often negative as positive. Preventing and eliminating definite evils —starvation, suffering, oppression, disease, poverty, and so on— often seem more urgent morally than promoting a positive good— education, self-determination, recreation, and so on. This is not to say that these and other positive goods are not important. They are; they constitute the life toward which we strive. But they cannot be sought where the minimal conditions of health and survival are not met. As Antony Flew underscores this idea, "Morally, so long as hospitals are needed, hospitals must have priority over amusement parks."[3] Literacy is important, but it is impossible to teach reading to people who are starving; meaningful work is necessary to a fulfilled life, but untreated serious disease precludes productive employment. Again, the point is that means and ends cannot be fully separated and isolated from one another.

Once doing our duty *regardless* of results is distinguished from achieving certain results *regardless* of what must be done to succeed in attaining them, priorities are clarified at the expense of polarizing a difference of emphasis into a radical difference in kind. This clean, total separation between means and ends, this mutual exclusion of each by the other, appears to be both *required* by the just-warist and *rejected* by the pacifist. It seems required to justify war because the just-warist grants the evil of the acts of war. Only if means and ends are totally separate can good consequences emerge from evil actions; otherwise the results would be spoiled by the evil means of achieving them. The split is rejected by all but the most extreme pacifists as an artificial, exaggerated dichotomy; means and ends, according to most forms of pacifism, are not separate but are merely different aspects of the event in question, aspects distinct in our naming them separately, but related as features of one action. One begins to move away from absolute pacifism as one begins to consider (to the slightest degree possible) the likely *consequences* of doing one's duty; one begins to move away from more extreme forms of just-warism (that is, those nearer to war realism) toward the weaker end of the pacifist continuum as one begins to wonder whether *any* and *all* acts are justified by a good end. The differences are real but are matters of emphasis and degree rather than radical distinctions in kind.

Different grounds for moral opposition to war and different models for positive peace warrant differing positions along the two pacifist continua developed below. Despite these differences, all but the most extreme pacifists are united in the conviction that means and ends cannot be separated cleanly. Of course the most extreme of absolute pacifists may hold that force is so intrinsically wrong that it must be avoided, whatever the consequence. But as we will see below, this position is rarely if ever actually held. It is part of the stereotyped caricature of pacifism that the warist presumptions of culture perpetuate and hold against pacifists who in fact do not hold the extreme view. To a pacifist along either the anti-war continuum or the positive peace continuum peace is not a separate and isolated objective or end to achieve but a policy to live. Ends and means coalesce.[4] It is just this commitment to the union of ends and means that seems to hold those along the pacifist continua together. But what of those along the just-war continuum? When peace is regarded as an objective to achieve, an end distinct from the policies that are the means of achievement, then the door is open to entertaining *any* and *all* means to gain so precious a goal, a goal on which pacifist and warist alike may agree. This is why the rhetoric of the warist can be so extreme: "Let every nation know, whether it wishes us well or ill, that we shall pay any price, bear any burden, meet any hardship, support any friend, oppose any foe to assure the survival and the success of liberty."[5] While this is an inspiring show of commitment to a worthy ideal, the pacifist wonders whether *any* price, burden, hardship, support, and opposition will be compatible with the goal. Can peace be achieved by warist means? Can freedom be achieved by oppressive means? Can trust be achieved by dishonest means? Can cooperation be achieved by coercive means? Can respect be achieved by threatening means? Can means and ends be sufficiently distinct, one from the other, to admit such disregard for consistency? At what point does disparity between means and ends manifest hypocrisy rather than exemplify commitment to moral action? These are not so much questions to be answered as efforts to establish the plausibility of the usual pacifist conviction that ends and means are integral one to the other.

In our consideration of the means/ends interrelationship it is important to recognize that moral issues, especially regarding whole nations of people, are complex and subtle, rarely simple matters of right and wrong. Commenting on what he calls word sickness in international communication, which he sees to be worsening since World War II, Thomas Merton points out the "unconscious aspiration to *definitive* utterance, to which there can be no rejoinder."[6] His reference is to

pompous and sinister jargon of war mandarins in government offices and military thinktanks. Here we have a whole community of intellectuals, scholars who spend their time playing out "scenarios" and considering "acceptable levels" in megadeaths. . . . They are scientifically antiseptic, businesslike, uncontaminated with sentimental concern for life. . . . One proves one's realism along with one's virility by toughness in playing statistically with global death.[7]

The ultimate danger of this language of finality is that anyone who disagrees is thereby wrong, negotiations are fruitless or not to be trusted, and governments resort to violence on the grounds that the adversary does not understand anything else. This sort of speaking and thinking precludes consideration of peaceful options by defining them out of existence. When the enemy is caricatured as incapable of understanding anything but violence, then only violence is a live option. Where the adversary "cannot be trusted" and dialogue is forsaken for manipulative rhetorical posturing, all words become unsure and the temptation to make one's meaning clear with blows becomes irresistible.[8] It is crucial to expose the language of finality because it helps create the context in which violence becomes the best or only option. The wrongness that the pacifist sees in war may be due to just this failure to choose another option, a less evil means. The judgment is not so much one of right versus wrong as it is a preference for better over worse, challenging the exaggerated extremes.

In exploring the means/ends dilemma in the ethics of war we have seen the pacifist insist on the inseparability of means and ends while the warist relies on a clean separation; but the warist too can recognize the inseparability of means and ends. It is the war setting that most often uses the board game model; the objective—victory—is separate and isolated from the means—strategy and tactics. Leaders weigh alternate routes to the same goal, sketching various scenarios; even the peacetime practices are called war games. Although there may be various ways to win military victory in specific wars, the means employed to a great extent determine the sort of victory achieved.

Consider how very different the [Allies'] victory of 1945 . . . might have been had the West adopted a rather different strategy earlier. By shifting weight from the front in France toward Italy and the Balkans, it might have been possible, at a price, to have won a significantly different victory. The Iron Curtain might then have enclosed less of Europe than it now does. The way you win a war determines the situation at the time of victory.[9]

Warists can know this; often the issue is whether the means of war are necessary to the end in question. And if the means are necessary but are themselves terribly evil, at what level is the evil of the means sufficient to provoke a consideration to forsake the goal?

To make a similar point in the arena of nuclear weapons one need only acknowledge that the nuclear age did not begin "exactly at fifteen minutes past eight in the morning, on August 6, 1945, Japanese time, at the moment when the atomic bomb flashed above Hiroshima."[10] Rather, "the Hiroshima and Nagasaki decisions were prefigured in Hamburg, Dresden, and Tokyo, in a policy of unconditional surrender, and in the desert of New Mexico."[11] To shift to the current arms race between superpowers, thermonuclear exchange begins not with the pressing of buttons or the turning of keys, not with the order to launch, but with the systematic, deliberate planning, development, and deployment of weapons designed to kill hundreds of millions of people, designed to reduce major seats of culture and civilization to radioactive rubble. The next war does not begin with the first shots but with policies of nations that threaten annihilation of other nations in an effort to preclude their own annihilation, that is, with threat, fear, counterthreat, counterfear, and so on. However hard we try to separate means and ends, the results we achieve are extensions of the policies we live; the means we choose reflect the sort of end we seek. Means and ends are aspects of one and the same event. Perhaps superpowers choose the means they do because they desire the inevitable threat/intimidation/domination outcome achieved.

We began this consideration of the means and ends of peace and war with familiar moral discourse and the exaggerated extremes to which pacifists and just-warists are driven as they try to justify actions. In considering the pacifist/just-warist opposition more carefully we begin to see pacifism and warism overlapping one another on the means/ends issue, agreeing, in part, on an inseparability of means and ends, disagreeing over the necessity of particular means and over the possible defeat of ends by terribly evil means. Perhaps a philosophical stumbling block in all of this is that we may be conceptually entrenched in a dichotomy of a traditional Western ethics, forced to choose between duty and results when trying to establish non-arbitrary and consistent foundations for morality. That is, perhaps the traditional division of normative ethics into deontological and teleological theories forces the dilemma. Once doing our duty *regardless* of results is distinguished from achieving certain results *regardless* of what must be done to succeed in attaining them, priorities are clarified at the expense of polarizing a difference of emphasis into a radical difference in kind.

Pacifists seize this interrelationship between means and ends to expose the logic of some just-war positions. Since war is never justified except as a necessary evil whose bad is to be outweighed by the good achieved, pacifists not only point out the inconsistencies between means and ends (war to end war, kill for peace, conscription to defend freedom, armed coercion to foster peaceful cooperation, and so on); they also point out the certainty of the evils undertaken as means and the uncertainty of achieving the good ends. All wars have losers as well as winners. The losers obviously do not achieve the ends that were to justify the horror of their means; thus their acts go without full justification. Sadly, even the winners may not succeed in gaining the ends that were to warrant their evil means; the actual victory in war rarely compares favorably to the result envisioned before and during the fighting. Perhaps this is why one lesson of the ages seems to be that, in war, everyone loses. The victors just lose a bit less than the vanquished. The pacifist point in pressing the interrelatedness of means and ends is underscored when we remember the claim that, although a moral person—and a moral nation—works both to accomplish positive good and to prevent and eliminate evils, preventing evil is always the more urgent as well as the less speculative objective.

If there is anything to the suggestion that the means/ends issue is an exaggerated opposition provoked by a polarized traditional conceptual framework where deontology (duty) and teleology (goals) are severed and separate, then perhaps this last pacifist critique of the just-warist view on the means/ends issue is better understood as a recasting of the issue. Here the pacifist point is to shift the moral burden onto the warist; the issue is not duty versus results but rather the relative degrees of certainty that the conditions of just war are met (*jus ad bellum*), that the means of war are undertaken justly (*jus in bello*), that the war in question is the *only* or *best* means to the end in view, and that the end in question is one that cannot be forsaken under any circumstances. The pacifist point is to suggest that the justificatory burden is the warist's and that it may not be possible to bear such a burden.

One of the many frustrations of the study of just-war doctrine is that "many commentators have garbled the original intent by approaching just-wars from the perspective of justifying violence."[12] But "in phrasing the question which leads to the celebrated just-war doctrine, St. Thomas shows his leaning toward peace. He does not ask when are wars moral or what are the conditions for a just war. Rather, St. Thomas queries sharply, "Whether it is always sinful to wage war.' "[13] Clearly the onus belongs on the warist; the presumption is that war is wrong. Further, since just wars can only be waged for peace, a search for peaceful alternatives to war must be undertaken prior to the outbreak of hostilities if the war in question is to be excused. Put frankly, "Only a leader who has pursued peace as steadfastly as our leaders have prepared for war could be said to possess the right intention prescribed for just war." [14]

The pacifist is even more critical of those defending policy through just-war doctrine, suspecting that genuine peacemaking is undertaken rarely by the modern sovereign state. What state asks whether it is always wrong to wage war? Clearly the contemporary presumption, as discussed in Chapter I above, is that a state can use any and all means it deems necessary to promote and protect its vested interests. Nations do not invest energy, money, time, and resources in peacebuilding at levels comparable to their investments in the means of war. Just-war doctrine has been used to excuse spending human, natural, and economic resources for warmaking at rates many times those of peacemaking and to justify the militarization of national priorities and economies while minimal efforts are directed to peace. Meanwhile, pacifists are ridiculed as hopelessly naive and even dangerous. The disproportionate commitment to the means of war would have to be reversed to show good faith in just-war doctrine. The point is that states rarely make the effort to show that war is the *only* or *best* means to the end in view; the presumption of warism precludes the need to do so.

Pressing this issue we recognize that states typically offer justifications for military intervention, citing self-defense, the need to aid allies in response to aggression or to protect their territorial integrity, the need to balance the interventions of others or to rescue victims of oppression. [15] Sometimes we do see states consider and even employ other means to achieve their ends: economic and cultural boycott, withholding economic, military, or technical aid, and so on. But these are usually preliminary steps, used to signal seriousness and often followed by threatened and actual military intervention. A large part of the reason that non-military means rarely get taken seriously as options is the dominant attitude that successful people and nations are tough, are not intimidated, do not give in or compromise when they can prevail. Hanna Arendt reminds us of this when she quotes Bertrand de Jouvenel: "A man feels himself more of a man when he is imposing himself and making others the instruments of his will," which gives him "incomparable pleasure.' " [16] While Arendt does not exploit the sexism obvious to our late twentieth-century awareness, her quotation is a blunt reminder of the extent to which cultural and political values reflect old stereotypes of macho men protecting the womenfolk. Unfortunately, the political values of our own day seem to lag behind even the modest reforms on the personal level. Sexism is not behind us on either plane, but it seems fair to suggest that the patriarchal and macho ideal has a stronger hold politically than interpersonally. At any rate, it is clear that states are eager to rationalize military means of achieving state objectives while typically neglecting the obligation to show that warism is the only or best means to the end in view.

The purpose here has been to examine the relationships between means and ends as they apply to attempts at justifying warmaking. We have seen that pacifism and warism seem to differ roughly along traditional deontological/teleological lines but that problems arise in trying to press the explanation too far because pacifists and just warists can agree on the interrelatedness of means and ends. It would be overstating the interrelationship to say that evil means can *never* contribute to good ends. Similarly, it would be an overstatement to claim that good means *always* produce good ends, that *whatever* means bring about good must thereby be good, or that *any* means contributing to an evil end must thereby be evil. The point has been to show that the means/ends relationship is not so simple as to allow these claims; yet there is just enough truth in each of them to keep us puzzled, wondering how to weigh our moral evidence, how to balance our moral desire to achieve the right thing with our moral duty to do so in the right way. Again the pacifist reminds us of the certainty of the means of any action and of the *un*certainty of the ends. This is why the immediate, clear, present case of personal self-defense from unprovoked personal attack is easier for the warist to justify, and harder for the pacifist to condemn, than is a distant, murky case of national military action to preempt potential aggression, done in the name of self-defense. In the former case the burden of proof seems bearable for the warist; in the latter, the burden seems too great to bear.

The ethics of international conflict involves a subtle and confusing set of issues complicated by innumerable variables and the interrelatedness of events. While it is important to reject moral skepticism in the international arena—the view that moral right and wrong are meaningless concepts when applied to policies and activities of nations—it is also necessary to avoid oversimplification. It is helpful to distinguish ends and means as we consider the dimensions of various problems and the range of options that may provide resolution. But we exaggerate the distinction into a radical separation when we talk glibly about ends so sacred that they warrant any and all means for their protection, or when we design, deploy, and intend to use weapons capable of putting an end to human life—and with it an end to any and all human goals.

Realizing that means and ends cannot be severed totally entails a genuine commitment to seeking means consistent with and appropriate to our ends. Realizing that pacifists and warists of various sorts can agree on the inevitable interrelatedness of ends and means provokes us to rethinking the theoretical differences between these seemingly polar opposite positions on the ethics of peace and war. And realizing the conceptual problems of overextending the deontology/teleology distinction encourages rethinking the traditional framework within which normative ethical positions are cast.

Another approach to understanding the range of normative ethical positions, one related to but different from the traditional deontology/teleology polarity, has emerged in recent feminist scholarship.[17] Carol Gilligan identifies two kinds of moral reasoning, one abstract and hypothetical, concentrating on rights and duties, the other contextual and narrative, focusing on responsibility and response. The former is based on viewing society as a collection of autonomous individuals constrained by rules to curb egoism and aggression. The latter rests on a concept of society as overlapping networks of mutual interdependencies where stability comes from a responsibility of care. The first is preoccupied with justice, the second with meeting people's needs. While these perspectives have strong associations with gender (the first male, the second female), they are clearly not dependent on gender. Most of us reason morally from both sets of values just as most of us are not purely deontologists or purely consequentialists. How we resolve conflicts between the demands of our sense of justice and the demands of our responsibilities for caring may expose our own moral priorities (just as whether we emphasize ends or means in the previous scheme does so). The expectation of universality—that there is one absolute right moral choice for any given moral problem—is once again called into question, this time by acknowledging the legitimacy of more than one perspective. Insisting that one must predominate means devising the principles for resolving any possible conflict between them.

Ethics has yet to arrive at a general consensus on resolving the dilemma of competing perspectives. Perhaps to do so would be to achieve greater precision than the subject will allow. The best we can do here is admit the problem, leaving the question open. There may or may not be one absolute universal right choice for every possible moral question. Granting that we do not *know* itself becomes reason for caution and tolerance. This is why the polarized extreme views are suspect. And this is also why the burden-of-proof issue is so important. Making war is doing massive, irreparable harm; doing such irreparable harm demands a very high degree of justification. But it is difficult to justify acts of such import without secure knowledge that they are warranted. And such knowledge eludes us in part due to the incompatability of ends and means in war and due to tensions between principle and caring.

The consideration of the ends/means complexities to moral reasoning has added to the difficulties faced by those trying to understand the morality of war. The lesson of recognizing such problems may well be that caution must guide moral judgments of war. The spirit of caution helps us appreciate the next step in exploring the moral continuum between warism and absolute pacifism, namely, the effort to examine and account for various positions along the pacifist segment of the spectrum.

CHAPTER IV

A PACIFIST CONTINUUM

Perhaps in pacifism, as in space, there should be no absolutes.

—Ronald W. Clark,
Einstein: The Life and Times

When cultural obstacles to taking pacifism seriously are set aside
—or, at least, acknowledged—and when the moral reasoning of
various warist positions has been explored, it becomes possible to
identify and examine a range of views falling within the parameters
of the general moral opposition to war as such. In this chapter
we will put aside discussion of the general pacifist commitment to
cooperative social conduct based on agreement and focus attention
instead on the variety of pacifist moral objections to war *per se*. This
is done because pacifist thought, at least concerning the anti-war

elements of pacifism, develops out of reaction to various attempts at moral justification of war.

We will consider a pacifist continuum or spectrum with relative positions along the scale resulting from varying reasons for the moral opposition to war. The purpose is not to present an exhaustive delineation and characterization of pacifist objections to war but to sketch stages along the continuum to establish the feasibility of understanding pacifism as a range of views distinct yet united. Examples will be offered at each stage, yet it will be left to the reader to imagine positions in the gaps between the views discussed. While references will be made to actual pacifists, the primary objective is not historical but theoretical. In fact most actual pacifists have expressed views at several points along the continuum; and a position along the scale can be perfectly legitimate as a variety of pacifism even if no widely known pacifist ever held the view.

At one end of the continuum is the absolute pacifism of the cultural stereotype described earlier. While few if any actual pacifists have held this view, it is the position often identified with pacifism. In its most extreme form, it is the view that it is wrong always, everywhere, for anyone to use force against another human being. Here force is understood to mean an imposition of physical strength.[1] The grounds for holding this position may vary widely. They may be deeply religious as in the later Tolstoy's rendering of Christian ethics, the period of "The Kingdom of God Is Within You" and his "Address to the Swedish Peace Congress in 1909":

> However much you may pervert the Christian teaching, however much you may hide its main principles, its fundamental teaching is the love of God and one's neighbor; of God—that is of the highest perfection of virtue, and of one's neighbor—that is of all men without distinction. And therefore it would

seem inevitable that we must repudiate one of the two, either Christianity with its love of God and one's neighbor, or the State with its armies and wars.[2]

Here absolute pacifism is the inevitable consequence of accepting God's Law. However, the same conviction can rest on secular moral principles as well, perhaps an interpretation of the practical formulation of Kant's categorical imperative where humans must always treat one another as having intrinsic worth—having dignity—and never treat one another as mere means to other ends.[3] Of course there could be other secular or religious doctrines that might be understood as requiring an absolute repudiation of all use of force between people; the point is that the absolute pacifist position need not rest on one particular set of grounds. Whatever the rationale on which it rests, absolute pacifism is difficult to defend. Persuading people to hold this view usually entails getting them to adopt a particular religious or metaphysical doctrine. Perhaps this accounts for the "conversion" experience stereotypically attributed to pacifists. As a result of the difficulty of being persuaded to absolute pacifism, and the rarity of anyone actually holding the view, it should be no surprise that "such principled versions of pacifism can be patronizingly tolerated by those who think them silly and/or dangerous."[4]

Absolute pacifism, understood as the position that any use of force between people is always and everywhere immoral, is widely regarded as "bizarre and vaguely ludicrous."[5] Objections to the view, popular and academic, tend to be *moral* objections. For example, Tom Regan argues:

Any view that would require that we judge, say, a woman who uses what physical power she has to attempt to free herself from an aspiring rapist, as having done, not, what might sometimes be the case, a foolish thing, but instead, and necessarily, an irredeemably evil act, must, I believe shock and offend the moral sensibilities of rational men.[6]

Regan concludes, "A person committed to an extreme pacifism . . . lacks a fully developed moral sensitivity to the vagaries and complexities of human existence."[7]

Two important points need to be made at this juncture. First, while highly unpopular among academics as well as the general populace absolute pacifism has both defenders and a plausible defense. Consider these words from Martin Luther King, Jr.:

> When, for decades, you have been able to make a man compromise his manhood by threatening him with a cruel and unjust punishment, and when suddenly he turns upon you and says: "Punish me. I do not deserve it. But because I do not deserve it, I will accept it so that the world will know that I am right and you are wrong," you hardly know what to do. You feel defeated and secretly ashamed. You know that this man is as good a man as you are; that from some mysterious source he has found the courage and the conviction to meet physical force with soul force.[8]

Acts of King and his followers demonstrated that moral strength can defeat physical force. Second, beyond the question of the correctness of the absolutist position is the realization that, while it is an important position, it is a serious mistake to think that it is the only version of pacifism. After all, it is obvious that one could prefer the position of Regan expressed above to that just quoted from King *without* giving up the general pacifist conviction that war, as such, is morally wrong. That is, one's view of the moral legitimacy of personal physical resistance to unprovoked, unjust personal physical attack does not necessitate a position on the moral legitimacy of *war*. It is reckless and sloppy thinking that identifies all pacifism with its most extreme version. Absolute pacifism is the end point on the proposed continuum of pacifist views; it does not embrace them all.

One reason that distinct versions of pacifism get blurred together is that people are often unclear about what violence is and how it is related to force, coercion, and power. These are large and crucial concepts. We will discuss and develop an understanding of them throughout our consideration of pacifism, but we do need at least provisional definitions here. We will take *violence* to be any physical act intending to injure, damage, or destroy a person or object. The term carries with it the notion of violation, a transgression, a wrongful invasion of persons or their personal realm. As mentioned above, force is the imposition of physical strength. Since force need not be undertaken with the intent to injure or destroy, force need not be violence, yet all violence would involve force. *Coercion* is an act intending to make someone do something that she or he does not want to do. It may involve force or violence or the threat of either, but it need not; one might coerce another by threatening to say something that the other would rather not be said.[9] *Power* is the ability or capacity to accomplish something.[10] The exercise of power may but need not involve force, coercion, or violence. A job supervisor, a teacher, a scientist, a parent might exercise the ability to get something done—that is, they might exercise power—quite independently of even the threat of force, coercion, or violence.

Sorting these out, even in this preliminary way, makes it possible to see that a pacifist may oppose violence—a violating action with the intent to injure or destroy—but need not thereby oppose force, the use of physical strength. Of course all war involves violence but not all violence involves war. Since pacifism is the moral opposition to war, there may be pacifists tolerating some instances of violence while opposing all war.

The first distinct step, then, along the spectrum away from the absolutist pacifist doctrine is the view that non-lethal force can be warranted in principle—for example, physical restraint for self-defense against unprovoked physical attack. This view is perfectly compatible with a general moral conviction that war, by its very nature, is wrong. For example, one might take a position like that of Leo Szilard, arguing that one should not destroy what one cannot create. Or one might adopt an interpretation of the Judeo-Christian commandment "Thou shalt not kill" that might exclude any and all homicide. These need not rule out physical resistance but they would exclude *lethal* "defense." Clearly the infamous "thug in the alley" attempt to reduce all pacifism to absurdity falls far short of its objective. A woman may be a pacifist (morally opposed to all war) yet use physical strength to resist abuse (our thug in the alley) without contradicting or compromising her principles. Depending on her variant of pacifism she may or may not compromise her principles by intending to injure her assailant. There are degrees of moral justifiability for the use of physical means to fend off attack.

Further along the scale is a view we might call collectivist pacifism, the position that it is possible in principle to justify even lethal violence while retaining the general pacifist objection to war. The view rests on the realization that one may oppose war, which always involves mass violence, while allowing a lethal self-defensive violence among individuals. A defense of this position involves arguing that it is possible for a human to perform an act so heinous that in so doing she or he forgoes any legitimate expectation to be treated as human. Extending the rationale that allowed backsliding from extreme pacifism, the argument would conclude that moral individuals are not required to treat sufficiently immoral persons by the ordinary standards of morality, that even the general principle requiring respect for human life might have exceptions. This would mean that in principle humans can somehow lose their right to life due to their own actions, that is, by doing something so evil that by doing it they give up their right to humane treatment. Of course, before taking action against anyone, one would need both a criterion setting the limits of human behavior and secure confidence that a given case is a genuine instance of breaching the criterion. This would be a very difficult burden of proof to bear, even in the case of a single individual. But we can imagine such a burden being met by marshalling the testimony of witnesses, incriminating physical evidence such as relevant fingerprints, and so on. Obviously the problems of establishing that masses of people had in fact committed acts by which they forgo their rights to humane treatment would be compounded incredibly by the numbers of people involved, especially in the confusing circumstances typical when war is feared.

It is clear that there is room for a great deal of disagreement on this substantive issue, whether the taking of a human life can be justified in principle and in fact. It is not for us to get lost in various versions of such arguments here. The point is that even pacifists might disagree about these matters. Those toward the absolutist end of the spectrum would reject any argument allowing the taking of even one life, however guilty of various crimes the victim may be. Those further along the scale might accept some reasons for taking a life; the specific conditions and safeguards against error might vary. Cautions of various sorts and to varying degrees would be required to guarantee that the decisions were made judiciously. This is not the concession to anti-pacifists that it might at first appear to be. While allowing the justifiability of lethal violence in even one individual case does open the door to the possibility of war being justifiable *in principle,* further stages along the pacifist continuum hold firm to the view that war cannot be justified *in fact;* and it is something about the very nature of war that precludes the justification in fact, not merely the absence of justifying conditions in a particular case.

Moving along the spectrum we reach what may be called fallibility pacifism or epistemological pacifism, the view that even if collective lethal violence can be justified in principle, still our knowledge is too limited to justify it in fact. Here the problems of scale mentioned above emerge in pacifist thinking. We simply cannot know relevant factors with sufficient confidence to warrant irrevocable violent actions between nations. On this view war is never justified, not because violence between humans is inherently wrong but because of inevitable limitations in our understanding of the facts and circumstances involved between large groups of people, because of the impossibility of knowing that the conditions of justification in principle indeed hold in fact. Given the subtlety and complexity of issues between nations, the history of tensions, the biases of involved parties, the propaganda, the vested interests, the manipulation of news media and events, the economic, political, geographic, and demographic inequities, our knowledge cannot be sufficiently secure to justify war, even if it were conceded that war is theoretically justifiable.

With this version of pacifism we have moved down the continuum away from basing the pacifist view on a concept of our duty toward basing it on the likely results of war. That is, the varieties of pacifism closer to the absolutist end of the scale put greater emphasis on principles concerning our moral obligations independently of consideration of likely consequences of our actions. Varieties of pacifism toward the opposite and weaker end of the scale are grounded in greater concern for anticipated results or effects of acts of war than on duties to which we are bound independently of consequences. Those at the former extreme think of war as wrong in principle, even if its effects could somehow be good; those toward the latter end of the scale might accept war in principle but reject it in fact because of the bad consequences entailed by war. Also, while the absolutist end of the spectrum has greater emphasis on the single human in principle, the opposite end of the pacifist spectrum puts greater emphasis on the collective human in practice. Fallibility pacifism may well be compatible with several varieties of just-warism but for one important exception: though the theoretical conditions warranting warfare may be agreed upon, the *knowledge* necessary and sufficient to justify acting in decisive, irreversible instances of war is wanting.

Examples of fallibility or epistemological pacifism are many. Gandhi uses these grounds frequently throughout his writing. This is one well-known instance: "Satyagraha is literally holding on to Truth and it means, therefore, Truth-force. Truth is soul or spirit. It is, therefore, known as soul-force. It excludes the use of violence because man is not capable of knowing the absolute truth and, therefore, not competent to punish." [11] Another: "Everybody admits that sacrifice of self is infinitely superior to sacrifice of others. Moreover, if this kind force is used in a cause that is unjust, only the person using it suffers. He does not make others suffer for his mistakes." [12] Along with a variety of other pacifist arguments in *The Fate of the Earth*, Jonathan Schell uses epistemological or fallibility pacifism as well:

Only a generation that believed itself to be in possession of final, absolute truth could ever conclude that it had reason to put an end to human life, and only generations that recognized the limits to their own wisdom and virtue would be likely to subordinate their interests and dreams to the as yet unformed interests and undreamed dreams of the future generations, and let human life go on.[13]

The fallibility pacifist needs sufficient evidence to get beyond reasonable doubt. On this view of pacifism, the complexities, subtleties, innumerable factors relevant to the knowledge required to regard a given set of conditions as an instance of the hypothetically justifiable war—the *jus ad bellum,* the just war—are simply beyond the rational confidence of even the best-informed citizen. Believing that war is justifiable is not enough to justify a war; one must *know* that the current situation qualifies as a just war. The fallibility pacifist believes that we can never be confident that we have achieved this knowledge.

Another version of pacifism further down the continuum can be called technological pacifism. It is the position that war itself may have been justified in the past, not only in principle but in fact, when volunteers believing in their respective causes met face to face in remote battlefields; but, the argument goes, the means of war in modern technological society have put the possibility of justifying war behind us. One's position on the historical distance of actual justified warfare is relative to the technological sophistication of the weaponry of the culture in question because overkill and increased risks to non-combatants, non-participants, and innocent bystanders go hand in hand with technological "advance." Even if the problems raised by the fallibility pacifist are met and all and only "deserving" individuals are targeted by a war effort, still, war in modern technological society is rendered unthinkable in moral terms because war between nations equipped with modern weaponry entails the wholesale slaughter of countless ordinary people who do not identify with the economic, ideological, or political stakes, yet find themselves caught in the crossfire.

In an articulate and widely discussed essay, "The Morality of Obliteration Bombing," Father John Ford questions the bombing of civilians, a "practice which can be called typical of 'total' war." [14] Recognizing that "the most radical and significant change of all in modern warfare is . . . the enormously increased power of the armed forces to reach behind the lines and attack civilians indiscriminately," Ford defines obliteration bombing as

> the strategic bombing, by means of incendiaries and explosives, of industrial centers of population, in which the target to be wiped out is not a definite factory, bridge, or similar object, but a large section of a whole city, comprising one-third to two-thirds of its whole built-up area, and including by design the residential districts of workingmen and their families. [15]

During World War II obliteration bombing was used to demoralize the enemy, to break the support of the citizenry, to erode societal willingness to fight on. Ford examines a variety of attempts to justify obliteration bombing (for example, "the enemy did it first," or "military necessity demands it," or "it is justified by way of reprisal," or "the present situation is desperately abnormal." Finding these reasons insufficient, Ford remarks that obliteration bombing would be regarded as clearly immoral were it not for the principle of the double effect, the distinction between actually intended and merely expected consequences of an action. The principle is central to just-war theory and not one Ford is willing to give up. But he sees the principle abused in the case of obliteration bombing. Concerning the deaths of civilians, the families of workers, the sick and elderly, even those who do not support the war stance of their own country, to say that such deaths are unfortunate, unintended by-products of the military effort is simply dishonest. The deaths of these very civilians are precisely the objective of obliteration bombing. As if this were not enough to settle the matter, Ford goes on to apply the principle of proportionality, a second central condition required by just-war theory. This principle excuses the evil of particular actions as necessary to a greater good; that is, the evil is defeated or outweighed by the good of the over-all objective achieved. Obviously this principle is very difficult to apply; projected goods and evils vary in likelihood of occurring in proximity, in degree, in quality, quantity, duration, and breadth of effect. At any rate, "the evil brought by obliteration is certain injury and death, here and now, to hundreds of thousands, and an incalculable destruction of their property. The ultimate good which is supposed to compensate for this evil is of a very speculative character."[16]

While Ford concludes that "it is possible for modern war to be waged within the limits set by the laws of morality, and that the resort to obliteration bombing is not an essential part of it," he grants that, if modern war necessarily includes such means, then it is necessarily immoral itself.[17] The technological pacifist holds that in fact modern war *does* necessarily include the wanton death and destruction of countless innocent people; such is expected and certainly disproportionate to any conceivable good to be achieved. Thus, on this view, modern war is immoral.

One might wonder what the technological pacifist would say about less than modern warfare. Were past wars justified or, at least, justifiable? Could modern nations wage sufficiently pre-modern warfare to meet the justificatory conditions? Opinions may range widely on answering the first question, though broad agreement would be expected that current and future wars are more pressing as moral problems than are wars that cannot be undone. On the second issue the technological pacifist would be expected to be highly doubtful that nations with the knowledge to build—or, at least, to gain access to—modern weaponry would refrain from resorting to such means of war should the situation become desperate enough. Expecting nations to fight limited wars when they are equipped for total war may rest on a confidence in moral restraint that history does not confirm. One of the lessons of the arms race over the centuries is that nations tend to do what their weapons make possible.

Since the ominous prospect of thermonuclear war exaggerates the concerns of the technological pacifist by powers of ten, the most common contemporary version of this stage on our continuum can be called nuclear pacifism. The difference in degree of the destructive potential of nuclear weapons as compared with conventional weapons forces us to recognize a different point along the proposed scale as well. All technological pacifists are nuclear pacifists, but not all those morally opposed to any and all uses of nuclear weapons need be technological pacifists, since some might endorse, for example, strengthening of conventional forces, even as a means to reduce the nuclear threat. As I understand the view, a nuclear pacifist would not support a buildup of conventional arms because she or he would recognize that the knowledge to build nuclear weapons cannot be undiscovered. As Jonathan Schell puts it:

> The fundamental origin of the peril of human extinction by nuclear arms lies not in any particular social or political circumstances of our time but in the attainment by mankind as a whole, after millennia of scientific progress, of a certain level of knowledge of the physical universe. As long as that knowledge is in our possession, the atoms themselves, each one stocked with its prodigious supply of energy, are, in a manner of speak-

ing, in a perilously advanced state of mobilization for nuclear hostilities and any conflict anywhere in the world can become a nuclear one.[18]

Of course most of what has been said here about nuclear weapons could also be said analogously about biological and chemical weapons; they too present ominous and unimagined destructive potential. The technological pacifist recognizes the relationship between the means of modern warfare and what has come to be the nature of war itself. While we can wonder about the possibility of justifying war in years long past, we no longer have the luxury to do so regarding contemporary war.

The technological factors go beyond the development of modern weaponry. Contemporary communications, surveillance, and transportation, coupled with the complex network of international alliances and the general interdependency of nations, all contribute to making the possibility of justifying any war quite remote. Even a "tribal" skirmish among so-called third-world peoples has the potential to widen into an international incident that might provoke armed hostilities at any level. The technological pacifist sees these conditions as hopelessly interconnected and thus is not inclined to expect the major and minor powers to remain aloof. On this view, the moral responsibilities of nations are relative to their capacities and potentials for immorality through warfare. Those nations capable of the wholesale destruction of entire population centers with the push of a few buttons have a heavier moral burden of proof to justify themselves than do guerrilla soldiers involved in civil wars in their homelands. This is not to claim that either can be justified or that both cannot; rather it is to say that the burden of moral justification of actions is greater in some cases than in others due to the implications of the differing acts of war. Since the acts will not be justified in themselves but as means to desired ends, the fullest account of potential consequences must be weighed against the probability of achieving the desired end. For example, the smaller scale, close proximity, clear and present case of self-defense, imaginable in a civilian-soldier's use of personal weapons against a colonial occupying force, is less obviously wrong, basing the moral decision on consequences, than a massive launch on warning of ICBMs bearing multiple thermonuclear warheads. Even if all war is morally wrong, still some wars may be more wrong than others. One might even imagine a moral-justification-burden curve resulting from plotting technological sophistication of the available means of warfare against the chances of justifying war based on consequences: the greater a nation's capacity for mass indiscriminant destruction, the greater its burden of moral justification for any military involvement.[19]

Another variation on technological pacifism is what may be called ecological pacifism. Here the concern goes beyond the human immorality to fellow humans and focuses on wrong done to nature; still grounding the moral opposition to war on likely consequences, the focus shifts from impact on humanity to impact on the environment. It is bad enough that humans should kill one another; it is somehow worse that they should risk the extinction of the human species along with culture, other animal and plant species, perhaps life itself. This is what Schell refers to as the "second death," an extinction of a *type* of being beyond the death of a particular being. As Aldo Leopold puts it in an entirely different context, "A thing is right when it tends to preserve the integrity, stability, and beauty of the biotic community. It is wrong when it does otherwise."[20] This is clearly a results-focused morality that regards modern technology as dangerously tinkering with a fragile and incredibly complex infrastructure. The worry is not merely that humans suffer when the environment is

abused; it is that the environment itself has value beyond its useful-
ness to humans. Recent publications of research findings concerning
the potential for what has come to be called nuclear winter combine
the ecological and nuclear pacifist concerns:

> Nuclear weapons, especially when detonated in the air, produce
> an intense thermal pulse that can ignite fires simultaneously over
> vast areas. Any city attacked with nuclear weapons will burn,
> and many of these burning cities will generate firestorms whose
> gigantic smoke columns will carry soot particles into the upper
> atmosphere, where they might linger for months before settling
> out. The pall of smoke from burning cities would rapidly diffuse
> over the mid-latitudes of the Northern Hemisphere and might
> circulate into the tropical regions around the equator, which,
> for complex reasons, would be even more sensitive to changes
> in ambient light and temperature. Darkness at the earth's sur-
> face would bring a decline in mean annual temperatures of as
> much as 40 degrees centigrade for months. If the war took place
> in spring or early summer, temperatures might fall well below
> zero throughout July, August, and September. For months it
> might be as dark at midday as it normally is on a moonlit night.
> The effects of this long, cool "night" on plant ecology—and
> everything that lives is ultimately dependent on the photosyn-
> thesis of plants—are hard to predict in detail but would almost
> certainly be catastrophic.[21]

Increasing awareness of the environment, its complexity, fragility,
interdependency, and the near irreversibility of environmental damage, contributes to the case for technological pacifism.

Finally, at the weakest extreme along the pacifist continuum,
perhaps on the cusp between pacifism and just-warism, we have

pragmatic pacifism, the view that, as a matter of fact, wars tend to promote, not relieve human misery. Committed to the greatest good for the greatest number of people, pragmatic pacifists stand alongside Utilitarian just-warists on the projected continuum. This is why the ranks of pragmatic pacifists diminish as the evil results of unchecked violence grow, and vice versa. The rise to power and influence of Hitler-like individuals shrinks the ranks of pragmatic pacifists; awareness of Vietnam-like "no-win" military quagmires swells these ranks. But while they are closely related concerning the desired ends, pragmatic pacifists differ from just-warists on the relations between means and ends. The former do not believe means and ends can be cleanly separated and thus reject the notion that violent means can achieve peaceful ends. The just-warist, on the other hand, defends war as a means to an end. One implication is that non-violent resistance may be used as a tactic by just-warists; one need not be a pacifist to use nonviolence.[22] In fact one common thread in the varieties of pacifism discussed—beyond the moral opposition to war *per se*—is this understanding that peace is not an isolated and separate objective to be reached but an end that subsumes its means. Although pacifist positions vary as emphasis shifts from principles of duty independent of possible results to moral judgment based on anticipated consequences, all but the most extreme absolute pacifists see peace as means and ends inextricably bound. When means and ends are regarded as separable, the pacifist continuum is left for varieties of warism, although some overlap is possible as seen above.

The position maintained here is not that everyone is a pacifist in her or his own way. Pacifists all regard war as immoral by its very nature. No one likes war, but many people believe that war can be morally acceptable, even morally required. They are not pacifists. Others might not regard themselves as pacifists (perhaps due to cultural stereotyping), yet on reflection they may in fact consider war as immoral by its very nature. They are pacifists as it is developed and understood here. Still others might oppose the arms race, stand against the very concept of limited nuclear war, question the very suggestion that nuclear weaponry superiority yields national security, and so on. If their views have moral foundations based on the nature of war, then they are flirting with the pacifist range of views. Seeking disarmament is opposing the capacity to push violence to its utmost bounds; that is, it is opposing the capacity for war. When opposition to pushing violence to its utmost bounds is based on the consideration that such would be morally wrong due to the nature of war, then the view is a legitimate version of pacifism. Trying to civilize international affairs by rejecting ultimate weaponry on moral grounds is to move onto the pacifist continuum.

Of course many people oppose war—especially nuclear war—on non-moral grounds. Their opposition is not based on considerations of right and wrong. They might reject war as destructive of their way of life, as unpleasant or disruptive, as personally threatening, or even as bad for business. Surely there are numerous sound but non-moral reasons to oppose war. These individuals—though perhaps committed to reducing the likelihood of war—are not flirting with pacifism in their anti-war sentiments. But when the grounds for anti-war sentiment are moral, and when it is war as such that they oppose, then it is the "ultimate arbiter of disputes" that is under attack; in short, it is pacifism of a sort that is being put forth.

Those who regard themselves as pacifists and those who reject pacifism might unite in resisting this characterization of pacifism. A good many of those who consider themselves pacifists might prefer a much narrower range of views as pacifist, perhaps limiting it to near the absolutist end of the continuum. By the time people make their way to the extreme moral duty end of the spectrum, they often consider pacifism to be a complete way of life centered on the strength of absolutist pacifist conviction, radiating outward from the individual to society. To them, the suggestion of a pacifist continuum might seem to be a watering-down, cheapening, even pandering a noble doctrine. Anti-pacifists as well might prefer a more stereotypic absolutist characterization of pacifism; it is harder to commit oneself to and thus limit the ranks of pacifists to a hard-core few who can be written off as fanatics. Intellectual, emotional, and moral strength are threatening to those who understand and deal primarily in physical strength. A broader range of legitimately pacifist views makes pacifism more difficult to dismiss. This ironic convergence of opposites suggests that there is much to be said for a continuum of pacifist views. In an era when political expediency encourages polarization of views, exceedingly complex and subtle problems can receive crude and simplistic treatment. The morality of war is not a simple choice between good and evil. There are degrees of each and they are reflected in varying degrees of support and opposition for "the decision by arms." Responsible decisions involve the investment of time and energy to understand sources of conflict. Even if one believes war can be justified, the better the relevant factors are understood, the less obvious is the right and wrong of any particular war.

While allowing a range of views is open to the charge of blurring the clear, kicking up dust and then complaining that it is hard to see, joining the worship of gray areas between polar extremes, the alleged clarity of oversimplification and stereotyping is artificial and misleading. The more we know the more we realize that things are much more complicated than we had imagined. This is a lesson we will continue to learn as we go on to discuss the varying conceptions of positive peace.

CHAPTER V

POSITIVE PEACE

The chief reason warfare is still with us is neither a secret death wish of the human species, nor an irrepressible instinct of aggression, nor, finally and more plausibly, the serious economic and social dangers inherent in disarmament, but the simple fact that no substitute for this final arbiter in international affairs has yet appeared on the political scene.

—Hanna Arendt,
On Violence

It is often said that the problem with the peace movement in the modern world is that it is just an anti-war movement. What is missing is a clear, *positive* vision of peace. Of course the same criticism can be made of those outside the peace movement; they too lack a clear, positive vision of peace. To existing powers in the modern

77

political arena, "peace is the continuation of war by other means," the time of intensive development of the techniques and technology of war.[1] Without a positive conception of peace we fall back into thinking peace is the absence of war and thus we are tempted to use any and all means necessary to preserve the *status quo*. Certainly this is a major problem of twentieth-century international politics. Change threatens established powers. Realizing that the mere absence of war is not genuine peace, we recognize our condition as cold war.

The policies of superpower nations have evolved to the point that we not only settle for cold war but actually intensify cold war in an effort to avoid hot war. As just-warist Michael Walzer describes deterrence, "We threaten evil in order not to do it, and the doing of it would be so terrible that the threat seems in comparison to be morally defensible."[2] Unfortunately, Walzer succumbs to the very temptation he warns us about. Regarding nuclear deterrence as criminal, Walzer accepts it "for the moment" as necessary, until "alternative ways to peace can be found."[3] Surely it is clear that for pacifists and just-warists alike, genuine positive concepts of peace are needed to provide options and offer alternatives to military means. It might be argued that this is among the most pressing needs of our era. Just as prevention of disease is preferable to any cure in medicine, so positive peace that prevents and precludes the eruption of war is preferable to unbeatable military might. As long as our best idea of peace is the mere absence of war, then peace is not real to us and relations between nations can only consist in war, the levels of intensity described on a temperature scale from cold to hot. At the coolest end we would find allies; the warmest possible to date would be nations engaging in thermonuclear war.

From the beginning, the description of pacifism offered here suggests a range of views involving two general convictions, each of which gets expressed in different forms by various pacifists. Pacifism is moral opposition to war *per se* and pacifism is commitment to cooperative social and national conduct based on agreement. A pacifist continuum was developed above to describe varieties of pacifist thought on the first general conviction. At this point we need to describe a range of views regarding the second general conviction.

The problem, bluntly, is knowing how to struggle against injustice without using violence. The primary injustices against which we must struggle are social oppression and economic exploitation among as well as within nations and the danger of military invasion between nations. The traditional response to invasion has been to threaten and use counterviolence. The traditional response to oppression and exploitation has been violent revolution.[4] The pacifist predisposition is to nonviolent methods of struggle because of the unavoidable interrelationship between means and ends described in Chapter III above. "If we desire a society whose institutions and habit patterns are non-violent, the means used must themselves not press for the reverse."[5] Seizing the need for means compatible with ends sought, the pacifist challenges the just-warist by rejecting the claim that war is a *necessary* evil. Since war is only justified by those who see it as a required means to an end, the pacifist counters with the suggestion that war is never the only means nor even the best means to a peaceful end. The goal is a world where institutions and organizations are not used to manipulate people for the glory and gain of others, where the use of physical force is always discriminate and never deliberately injurious, where conflict is resolved without resort to violence, where gross imbalances of personal, social, national, or economic power do not exist unchecked.[6] Put simply, the goal is a world of people and nations in control of themselves from within by agreement and cooperation rather than controlled from outside themselves by threat, coercion, intimidation, and domination. To create such a world, to work toward real security, "we must stop trying only to avoid war, and must start trying to achieve peace."[7] Because so little effort has gone into understanding what this means, in comparison with the efforts at efficient warmaking, we have entered the most difficult aspect of the morality of peace and war.

Perhaps the first step in the discovery of peaceful means to peaceful ends is the recognition that many nonviolent behavior patterns are regular features of modern society even though it is far from the more ideal world just described.

Wherever channels of discussion remain open; parliamentary bodies genuinely deliberate; courts adjudicate under specified rules of law; citizens are consulted about the formation of public policy; the police use physical force, if at all, only in a discriminating and non-injurious way; and problems of social justice occupy a central place in political discussion—wherever conditions of this kind obtain, fundamentals of non-violence, both as means and ends, already exist. Naturally, the exponent of non-violence will seek to sustain and expand such patterns.[8]

Just as war exists to varying degrees, warists justify wars to varying degrees; and as pacifists oppose war to varying degrees, so people are committed to nonviolent methods of struggle against injustice to varying degrees. Some of us are eager to exploit conditions that can be manipulated to justify violence while others are less anxious to abandon hope for negotiation, compromise, or other settlement that avoids violent confrontation. Just as anti-war sentiments differ with varying grounds for moral rejection of war, positive peace sentiments differ with varying expectations of successful resolution of problems. The point is that options to violence exist and are in use already;

the challenge is to make the options obvious, attractive, increasingly successful, and even habitual.

There have always been—will always be—tensions, divisions, conflicts of interest between individuals, families, groups, nations. While we can minimize these as causes of war, we will not likely abolish them because they seem

> rooted in the brute facts of human individuality, diversity, and self-concern. Since these facts are unalterable, the whole human scene and all human relationships are inevitably infected with divisiveness. . . . The only way to work positively for peace is by cultivating a sense of unity that is strong enough to contain this pervasive tendency to divisiveness.[9]

Although divisiveness can keep humans at odds with one another, inhibiting cooperation and obstructing agreements, the diversity of individuals that prompts divisiveness also affords the richness and variety that can yield constructive relationships.

All social life consists in a complex of individual persons, groups, members, sub-groups, each at once both whole and part as it relates to others. People form groups as "nations, races, economic classes, institutions, professional castes, local regions, families, and others" and the groups and individuals are interrelated in an extremely complex vertical and horizontal set of interactions. As a whole, each element—group or individual—"has an inner cohesion and character, pursues its particular purposes, and acts to protect its own interests."[10] As a part, each is both dependent on others and has others dependent on it. Each individual, group, institution, family, nation has its own interests to further and self to preserve; yet each must respond to the interests of its parts or members as well as respond to the whole of which it is part. "The entire human scene is an intricate field in which the forces of mutuality and divisiveness encounter one another in constantly shifting patterns." [11]

Peace—agreement-making—is manifest where the sense of community, of mutual interests, of shared purposes, somehow prevails over the divisiveness of conflicting interests, opposing purposes, disunity. This is why people of common origin and heritage, those sharing values or traditions, those familiar with one another through family, ethnic, institutional, or regional relationships find it somewhat easier to be at peace with one another than with those of differing values, backgrounds, and ancestry.[12] Peace, agreement-making, getting along by self-control from within a context rather than by the imposition of order from without, comes more naturally where the individuals, groups, or institutions are or seem to be alike than where they seem foreign to one another. In our modern world it is the heightened sense of nationalism that both pulls individuals together into states and keeps them at odds with those outside their states. While population growth, communications, transportation, economic interdependency, and numerous other factors encourage a global village vision of our world, fear, competition, and dogmatic political and religious ideologies exaggerate differences and exacerbate tensions. The pacifist sees promise as well as threat in these conditions.

Beyond likeness, understanding tends to bring people together, ignorance separates them. Knowledge gives us a sense of participation, a sense of belonging, a sense of familiarity; ignorance, on the other hand, makes us feel estranged, foreign, distant.[13] The more we know about a nation, culture, or individual, the better we understand its interests and actions. With understanding comes a reduction in fear, by degrees, as we gain confidence in predicting relationships between behavior and its conditions, between events and their contexts. Making peace involves maximizing the sense of participation, minimizing the sense of estrangement. This means promoting mutual understanding to break down barriers of cultural and physical distance and to ease tensions of religious, racial, ethnic, and historic sorts.

A pacifist vision of positive peace must offer both a general ideal at which actions will aim and particular methods by which the ideal is implemented. Of course the methods, as means, must be compatible with the ideal sought; and the ideal, as an ideal, will be a goal toward which we strive without expecting fully to succeed. One important consequence of seeing pacifism as a range of views is that, while it is morally good to choose the life of pacifism, it is not necessarily morally wrong not to do so.[14] As we have seen, this is because the pacifist continuum is based on differing grounds for moral opposition to war, the opposition based not always on absolute right or wrong but on what is better or worse. All pacifists are convinced that there are better—less wrong—options to the acts of war, even to those fulfilling the conditions of just-warism. The warist's mistake is in choosing the less morally desirable option. Pacifism is a set of ideals and actions to live by and strive for, not a moral requirement demanded of everyone. Not all pacifists demand pacifism of everyone because not all pacifists hold the position that pacifism is a moral duty. At the same time, all are convinced that the world would be better were more of us pacifistic. Just as we have seen degrees of conviction to the anti-warist aspect of pacifism, so here we see a range of views constituting a positive conception of peace. And as with the anti-warist scale, the positive peace scale too requires both a unifying ideal and a range of methods of implementation.

In describing the pacifist ideal of the positive vision of peace we take our lead from the complex interrelatedness of individuals and wholes just described. The challenge is to foster a sense of community, a sense of participation sufficiently strong to overcome the divisiveness and estrangement of competing interests, cultural differences, and misunderstanding. Working backwards from the self toward the positive peace ideal, we see human individuals often at peace first with parents and immediate family, next with kin or clan, then with home region or village, later with state or nation, ethnic group, race, religion, national allies, and so on. This is not always so, since a host of factors can alienate individuals from their parents, family, nation, and culture. But it is often so, since the opportunity for understanding is natural to the close proximity and familiarity of those with whom we first identify. It comes through different efforts with those less familiar, those foreign and unknown. The highest ideal is to see every human as a kindred being, to see nature itself as a home to live in, not as conditions to conquer. No doubt this can be caricatured as a sentimental image of the human family, a romantic, unrealistic fantasy of friendly nature; but the widening of one's moral vision, and with it the widening of one's sense of community, beyond the immediate and familiar, is the guide toward the harmonious and cooperative internal order characteristic of a peaceful world. The self—and with it the self-interest—of the individual person, institution, or nation is not sacrificed. Rather, it is pursued within a consciousness of the whole. This sense of global community is fostered by seeking and emphasizing interrelatedness among peoples, institutions, religions, races, and nations while at the same time resisting the narrow and divisive self-interest served by preoccupation with and polarization of differences. The harmonious ideal is anchored by a spirit of tolerance and respect where differences are seen as enhancing, broadening, and deepening the possibilities for human experience rather than as threats that must be destroyed or dominated.

One of the fascinating features of this peace, when it happens, is that it rarely occurs to those living peacefully that it is peace that they are making. They take it for granted. It is habitual. It is simply how they live and interact with one another. All of us succeed at this to some degree, perhaps with close friends or immediate family, perhaps with co-workers, with co-members of a team or organization, with neighbors or customers or even those unknown people with whom we share the highways as we drive, in any context dependent on cooperative behavior.

Unfortunately, there are limits to the breadth and strength of any sense of community and, as a result, it seldom occurs to us to take this same peacefulness for granted as the way to interact with every and any person. Our ignorance and fear, our impatience and intolerance get the best of us to varying degrees under varying conditions. Some of us are more narrowly self-interested and intolerant, even bigoted and disrespectful of a range of cultural types and points of view. Others have broad and deep commitments to variety, diversity, differing values and perspectives. Of course there are those who take narrow advantage of peaceful others, not fully respecting or understanding the broader advantage to all of genuine peace. Criminal activity often manifests intolerant imposition of will and coercive domination of victims without regard for the victims' interests. Those who rupture the peace must be dealt with. The mark of truly peaceful people is whether their methods of dealing with peace-breakers are consistent with their visions of peace.

Everyone has many senses of community relative to the many sets of interrelationships in which we find ourselves. Inevitably, the breadth and strength of some communities are forged at the expense of others. We encounter conflicts of loyalty and we make choices: parent over friend, our nation over others, our religion over a national policy, our nation above all, our self above all, the reverse to any or all of these, and so on. The positive peace ideal pulls us to attempt orchestrating these conflicting loyalties into harmony by appealing to the broadest possible community and asserting that the good of the whole is to the ultimate advantage of each (rather than the reverse). Examples can be found in virtually any pacifist literature: Leo Tolstoy's family of God, Jane Addams' internationalism, Albert Schweitzer's sanctity of all life, Mohandas Gandhi's satyagraha, Albert Einstein's reverence for nature, Martin Luther King, Jr.'s law of unconditional love, Dorothy Day's atonement with the poor, Bertrand Russell's "remember your humanity, forget the rest," Adolfo Pérez Esquivel's voice of the marginalized and the disappeared, and others. The point is always to build on and broaden the sense of community by stressing interdependence, respect, tolerance, common aspirations, and understanding.

Our condition of conflicting loyalties can be exploited by exaggerating differences and building a stronger narrow community at the expense of wider ties to the whole human community. Bigots and demagogues of various types prosper by heightening our fears of the unfamiliar and polarizing people into "us" and "them." Pacifists retain hope for broadening the sense of respect, cooperation, and understanding in spite of the exploitation of differences. One reason for this is a paradoxical feature of peace: "It thrives best in those contexts where individuals and groups stand in several different and conflicting relationships with one another." [15] Those working at cultural and educational exchanges, trade agreements, travel opportunities, and other contacts between traditional adversaries help to widen and strengthen the sense of community and cooperation by the proliferation of contacts and relationships between parties. It is hard to overlook common values, interests, even common problems, when your nation's enemy is your customer, your source of goods and entertainment, your host, your guest. Expanding interrelatedness across traditional sovereign state boundaries can check narrow nationalism and foster internationalism. In Camus' words, "We are asked to love or to hate such and such a country, such and such a people. But some of us feel too strongly our common humanity to make such a choice." [16] The pacifist's task is to understand and foster those strong feelings of common humanity.

Where the idea of a cooperative community of nature, of humanity, of life, of the whole, is set as an ideal, activities of life that foster and manifest the ideal are internalized as patterns of behavior. They are nonviolent because violent behavior always ruptures the sense of community and is incompatible with an internally ordered whole. Of course the most obvious nonviolent method to resolve conflict and achieve agreement is discussion. Given the complex and diverse interests that characterize all human individuals and institutions, we cannot expect talk to succeed every time in establishing agreement. Sometimes talk itself is used destructively to manipulate, to attempt forcing submission. Where people and groups cannot work out agreements by discussion, resolution might be achieved by appeal to an impartial third party. Personal, family, town, state, corporate, national, church, and international rules, policies, and procedures, all provide means for arbitration and settlement. But some conflicts do not get resolved satisfactorily even in these various legal arenas. "Conflicts which, in one way or another, involve the fundamental principles of a society, of independence, of self-respect, or of a people's capacity to determine their own future" sometimes can be resolved "only through struggle." [17] The challenge to pacifism is providing alternatives to both violence and surrender.

Methods of nonviolent peacebuilding cannot get complete delineation here. In *The Politics of Nonviolent Action*, Gene Sharp cites nearly two hundred techniques, all nonviolent and thus compatible with the peaceful world that is our end. All are ways to confront power by appealing to the vulnerability of power: the consent of the ruled to be ruled. Withdrawing that consent can erode or destroy the power some have over others. A brief sketch of the range of nonviolent means of struggle will fill out the vision of positive peace by showing its implementation. Sharp categorizes nonviolent actions into three types, each beyond discussion and arbitration, each successively closer to physical confrontation. The first category beyond varieties of arbitration consists in efforts of political protest and persuasion, symbolic acts demonstrating opposition or support. Personal and group letters, petitions, lobbying, picketing, wearing symbols, marches, singing, mock funerals, and teach-ins are all examples of this level of struggle. Beyond protest and attempts at persuasion are methods of non-cooperation. Social and economic boycotting, strikes, slow-downs, withholding funds, reporting "sick," walk-outs, domestic and international embargoes, all serve as instances. Beyond non-cooperation are methods of nonviolent intervention. These include sit-ins, fasting, formulation of shadow governments, underground newspapers and radio, as well as various acts of civil disobedience. While Sharp does not present them explicitly as such, these can be seen as acts along a spectrum from cooperative discussion through arbitration, protest, and non-cooperation to nonviolent intervention. The next step would be to violent intervention, leaving the pacifist range of peacebuilding options. Just as pacifists may fall at any point along the continuum of views regarding the opposition to war, so pacifists may take differing positions along this spectrum of nonviolent actions. There seems to be no necessary link between positions taken on the two scales.

For the pacifist, leaving the nonviolent range of peacemaking options is tantamount to surrender, for it amounts to betraying one's ideals in pursuit of them. But perhaps this is too quick. As we saw above, there are legitimate versions of pacifism where a small-scale, personal resort to violence, while never desired, might be excused by some pacifists under restricted conditions. But even if violent acts between individuals can be condoned by some pacifists in exceptional situations, still no pacifist can resort to war; the restricted excusing conditions simply cannot be met in large-scale group interactions.[18]

The methods of nonviolent action have been used throughout history, sometimes because the means of violent struggle were unavailable or insufficient to meet the strength of opponents (that is, pragmatic pacifism), other times due to the moral preferences of those in the struggle (that is, the more principled rather than consequentialist versions of pacifism).

American colonists used nonviolent resistance in their struggle against Britain, refusing to pay taxes and debts, refusing to import, refusing to obey laws they considered unjust, using independent political institutions, and severing social and economic contact with both the British and pro-British colonists. . . . In the late nineteenth and early twentieth centuries, working people in many countries used noncooperation in the form of strikes and economic boycotts to improve conditions and to gain greater power.[19]

Gandhi's nonviolent campaign for Indian home rule and Martin Luther King's use of nonviolent activism to win greater respect for the civil liberties of blacks are other obvious examples. Clearly, nonviolent action has been used, often with success, in domestic as well as international conflict. This is despite the overwhelming efforts that have gone into research, development, and training in the means of violent conflict while very little effort has gone into making nonviolent action an effective substitute for violence.[20] The choice is not between passive submission and violence. Nonviolent action offers a wide range of options to avoid both.

While it is often granted that nonviolent methods can achieve victory in domestic social and economic struggles, nonviolence is rarely taken seriously when it comes to national defense. It is at this point that a special effort at setting aside social preconceptions seems in order. As Martin Benjamin suggests, "It is a mistake to suppose that there is no plausible way to defend a nation's security apart from the actual or threatened infliction of bodily harm to aggressors or potential aggressors."[21] In fact, non-military defense not only may be plausible but also may be more likely effective in achieving security goals than the superpowers' present means of stockpiling nuclear weapons and threatening nuclear holocaust. As Richard Barnet points out, "The result of this gigantic investment in security has been to make the American people among the most insecure on the planet."[22] In raising the arms budget while leveling or reducing budgets for health care, for environmental protection, and to fight crime and poverty, Americans express increasing *in*security. Ironically, we "are becoming less secure not only in spite of our continued disproportionate reliance on military means of national defense, but also *because* of this reliance."[23]

Gene Sharp presents an articulate and concise description of civilian-based nonviolent defense in his essay, "Making the Abolition of War a Realistic Goal."[24] Sharp points out that advocates of strong defense are stubborn and persistent "in considering only military means and failing to investigate nonmilitary possibilities," thus leading to the present dangerous situation and to the neglect of development of options. Based not on military weapons and troops but on societal strength, civilian-based nonviolent defense would use prepared civilian nonviolent action to preserve a society's freedom against external invasion and occupation. The point is to make domination and control by an external force impossible. This is achieved by "massive and selective nonviolent noncooperation and defiance by the population and its institutions." The attackers find the populace unrulable and are denied their objectives. Rather than converting opponents, expecting them to be persuaded to pacifism, nonviolent civilian struggle disrupts, paralyzes, frustrates opponents by denying the cooperation needed; invaders would not realize the gains expected. Teachers, clergy, government, and news media personnel and the general population would resist attempts at indoctrination and refuse to cooperate with efforts to introduce the invader's propaganda. Boycotts, strikes, non-cooperation by all levels of labor and management would diminish or preclude economic gains sought by attackers. Professional groups and trade unions would delay and withhold essential knowledge and service. The invading force would come to see the occupation as more trouble than it was worth.[25]

It is foolish to pretend that there would be no casualties with civilian-based nonviolent defense. As with military struggle, casualties are to be expected. It would seem that casualties in civilian struggles are typically lower than in conventional war; the struggle for black civil rights in the sixties, while costly in lives and injuries, would have been much more bloody with many more deaths had it been a violent revolt. Certainly nonviolent civilian-based defense casualties would pale when compared with losses in thermonuclear exchange. Civilian-based nonviolent defense has the additional benefit of strengthening a society during peacetime because it depends on the integrated cooperation of all segments of cultures in the systematic refusal to capitulate to invading forces. Beyond this, it must be recognized that a country trained in and dependent upon nonviolent civilian defense, a country without massive conventional and nuclear armaments and armies, is far less likely to be feared by other countries as a potential invader, and thus far less likely to be targeted by them.[26] A country with civilian-based nonviolent defense is a country without offensive military capability and thus much less a threat to others.

Security comes with cultural stability and freedom from fear. Amassing arms for protection against possible invasion from without provokes others to do the same. Not wanting to be bullied, each side tries to gain arms superiority; thus offensive weapons are multiplied and everyone is less secure, less free from fear. The cycle is repeated. Modern technological societies have driven the arms race to a point where the means of our security are the means of our insecurity. As dangerous as this situation is, it does have the consequence of prompting a rethinking of the means of defense and encouraging a genuine search for effective alternatives to traditional warism.

It is obvious that no nation can convert instantly from dependence on traditional military defense to civilian-based nonviolent defense. Nations have gotten into the present predicament in small but steady increments and the most likely route away from warism and the arms race would also be incremental. It will take time, but each step will ease the current dangers. It will take determination, but confidence is built by modest yet persistent gains. It will require exposing cultural predispositions to warism and it will take a socialization to peace-making across all segments of culture. These too will come slowly in stages rather than by miraculous conversion from one extreme to the other. The pacifist continuum and the range of nonviolent actions both allow a gradual backing away from warism, a backing into pacifism. Seeing peace and war to be related by these gradations makes possible a spectrum of practical alternatives so that the arms cycle need not be pursued beyond the brink.

It is obvious that even a gradual transarmament from traditional dependence on conventional and nuclear weapons to civilian-based nonviolent defense will require a generous transfusion of pacifism—both in the anti-war and in the positive peace formulations—into all aspects of culture, especially including public and private education. Perhaps this will begin with recognizing our cultural presumption of warism and with reclaiming the lost and neglected history of nonviolent action. Similar efforts have been important to recover lost, repressed and neglected racial and cultural minority history, as well as to correct gender-biased language and role definition. While progress is painfully slow in these areas, progress is being made and it directly affects the lives of many. Slow as it may be, progress at becoming aware of and backing away from warism will also transform our foundation values and will directly affect all of our lives.

The implications of the moral continua on peace and war described here may stretch beyond our powers of imagination, just as President Lincoln may not have imagined black congressional representatives and senators, or black candidates for the presidency, when he made the Emancipation Proclamation. But before attempting to explore the implications of the moral continua on peace and war and before entertaining the prospects for backing away from warism, we must first turn to consider the more familiar objections to pacifism, objections so common that they often preclude taking pacifism seriously at all. These constitute a stock or standard supply of criticisms anticipated by anyone inclined to sound at all pacifistic in modern culture.

CHAPTER VI

OBJECTIONS

Pacifism, with all the sympathy that it might inspire, is a clear example of naiveté.

—Risieri Frondizi,
"The Ideological Origins of the Third World War"

Anyone who has taken pacifism seriously knows the standard objections to pacifism. Entertaining pacifist thoughts means being prepared repeatedly to face questions about reacting to a mugger and confronting Hitler as well as about being realistic, self-righteous, and self-sacrificial. Cultural predispositions encourage an almost automatic response to pacifism, nearly always negative, often thrown out in a flippant or sarcastic way, suggesting that only a dupe, not a thoughtful human being, could even consider pacifism.

Perhaps the most effective forms of refutation of any idea are neglect and ridicule. Certainly these are the most common reactions to pacifism. Of course these are not true refutations at all; rather, they are often successful ways to evade having to take pacifism seriously. We might wonder why it is more tempting to elude than engage pacifism. Part of the reason may be the aura of moral strength that surrounds pacifism in spite of the hostile cultural climate. This aura is secured by the very few but respected and effective well-known pacifists even though their pacifism is culturally suspect and their successes often are explained away. Surely neglect and ridicule are encouraged by dominant cultural values; perhaps pacifism raises such fundamental questions that many of us fear the unsettling consequences of a genuine confrontation between our own behavior and ideals. Whatever the reasons, pacifism draws more hostile derision than careful criticism.

It is not possible to defend any value position from ridicule. Those mocking a given moral perspective are thereby refusing to take it seriously. A pacifist cannot be defended from the charge of being naive, utopian, or hopelessly romantic. Namecalling is definitive utterance that admits of no defense, other than simple denial. It is disappointing how often one finds namecalling, sarcasm, and condescending tolerance toward pacifism in otherwise serious discussions of practical and moral problems of war and peace. Awareness of the cultural predisposition to warism and the resulting prejudicial climate in which pacifism must be discussed frees us to consider substantive criticisms.

Turning to more genuine objections to pacifism, the vast majority of standard criticisms are variations of "BE REALISTIC." These tend to be expressed with remarks like, "pacifism sounds good but it just won't work" or "I agree in theory but not in practice." Since practical objections can only be resolved by reference to empirical evidence, it is at this point that the long history of nonviolent action needs to be known. People tend to think pacifist action will not work because they are largely ignorant of where and when it has worked. In fact, nonviolent action has been an effective and widespread means for social change, defense of rights, resistance against invasion, improvement of economic conditions, and overthrow of dictators. While a thorough history of nonviolent action cannot be included here, brief sketches of selected successful pacifist direct actions will be helpful.[1]

Examples of effective use of nonviolent action can be documented at least as far back as fifth century B.C. Rome. Evidence is scattered but "nonviolent action certainly occurred between Roman times and the late eighteenth century, when the case material becomes rich."[2] While many effective nonviolent actions are familiar, many more are neglected in our school history texts, or their significance is overshadowed by detailed accounts of battles, tactics, and acts of military heroes. Some effective nonviolent actions are recounted with little recognition that they fostered major social change without resort to violence. Instances of the effective use of nonviolent action from early American history include organized colonists challenging British rule by economic resistance, abolitionist struggles against slavery through boycott of slave-labor produced goods and support of runaway slaves via the Underground Railroad, the fight for women's suffrage through protest, civil disobedience, and tax resistance, as well as numerous strikes, boycotts, slow-downs, and protests characterizing the defense of workers' rights in the labor movement. Similar examples can be drawn from the histories of many other nations.

To a large extent, nonviolent means of struggle have replaced physical attacks, riots, and killings as means of social and economic reform, but we now take these nonviolent methods for granted as appropriate means for redress of economic and social grievances.

Unfortunately, we rarely recognize the role of nonviolent activists in the transformation of culture from violent to nonviolent means in achieving social and economic justice. When faced with the objection "it won't work," the pacifist response must be, simply, that nonviolent action does work and has a history to document the claim.

Serious critics of pacifism press further, objecting that while a few instances of effective use of nonviolent action have occurred, they are exceptional cases. To respond to this, pacifists need only underscore the innumerable cooperative acts undertaken routinely every day by the vast majority of people within any society. When this point is granted, the objection turns to require examples *not* from domestic conflict over economic or social grievances but instances where nonviolent struggle is "a major or predominant means of defense against foreign invaders or internal usurpers."[3] Here again history provides us with examples of successful nonviolent action. They include:

German strikes and political noncooperation to the 1920 Kapp *Putsch* against the Weimar Republic; German government-sponsored noncooperation in the Ruhr in 1923 to the French and Belgian occupation; major aspects of the Dutch anti-Nazi resistance, including several large strikes, 1940–45; major aspects of the Danish resistance to the German occupation, including the 1944 Copenhagen general strike, 1940–45; major parts of the Norwegian resistance to the Quisling regime and the occupation, 1940–45; and the Czechoslovak resistance to the Soviet invasion and occupation, 1968–69.[4]

It must be kept in mind that in these cases nonviolent actions were undertaken with success yet with little or no preparation, training, or planning. Of course the Czechoslovak resistance ultimately failed, "but it held off full Soviet control for *eight months* . . . which would have been utterly impossible by military means."[5] We can only speculate about how much more successful nonviolent defense would be were nations to prepare for it with the commitment of resources and energy at levels comparable to current investment in military defense.

When the most widely recognized and most successful examples of nonviolent struggle are cited—that is, Gandhi's campaign for Indian home rule and King's struggle for racial equality in America—the practical critics of pacifism unite in belittling the effectiveness of nonviolence. These successes, it is said, do not count for much because they were achieved against relatively civilized people, the British and the Americans; the suggestion is that against less moral and thus more formidable adversaries the techniques of nonviolence would surely fail. This line of argument is quite common even among the most respected social and political thinkers. According to Hanna Arendt, for example, "If Gandhi's enormously powerful and successful strategy of nonviolent resistence had met with a different enemy—Stalin's Russia, Hitler's Germany, even prewar Japan, instead of England—the outcome would not have been decolonization, but massacre and submission."[6] Michael Walzer, in *Just and Unjust Wars*, relegates consideration of nonviolence to an "Afterword," an appendix tacked onto but outside of his text. He grants that nonviolent resistance "has had a certain limited effectiveness" but he cautions that even this is possible only when the enemy shares the basic moral code of the civilian defenders. "When one cannot count on the moral code, nonviolence is either a disguised form of surrender or a minimalist way of upholding community values after a military defeat."[7] In "Pacifism: A Philosophical Analysis," Jan Narveson allows that "pacifism might work against some people" (he too suggests the British, noting that they are "comparatively nice"). But he warns that "the Nazis were apparently just 'egged on' by the 'pacifist' attitude of their victims."[8] This is a common line of argument in accounting for pacifist effectiveness while holding to the dominant cultural predisposition to warism. It merits careful consideration.

Perhaps because the history of nonviolent struggle is largely neglected or minimized in traditional school curricula, the popular notion prevails that Gandhi had a relatively easy time convincing the British to grant independence to India. It is widely recognized that Gandhi fasted a bit, led a few protest marches, and was arrested more than once, but the details are not widely known. Rarely is there acknowledgment of British brutality.

According to William L. Shirer, who discussed the issue personally with Gandhi, the "turning point" in the relations between the Indian people and their British rulers was the Amritsar Massacre, April 13, 1919, "the cold-blooded slaughter by the British of unarmed Indians gathered for a peaceful meeting."[9] Finding it hard to believe that the British had deliberately undertaken a mass killing of innocent people, and stunned that the act had received approval from most of the English in India and many at home (including the House of Lords), Shirer traveled to Amritsar in the early 1930s to better understand what had happened. As he tells it, "One had to see the physical layout of the Jallianwalla Bagh, the small public meeting place into which several thousand peaceful unarmed Sikhs, Hindus and Moslems had jammed that spring day of 1919; and one had to know why they had gathered there."[10]

India had been under British rule since the middle of the eighteenth century. During World War I, India furnished the British Empire over one million troops, suffered 106,000 casualties, and contributed nearly a billion dollars to the British cause, expecting independence in return. They received only a vague promise of gradual development of self-governing institutions.

When they realized that they had been deceived they reacted with some violence from one end of the country to the other. To repress the outbreak the British . . . instituted virtual martial law in much of India and deprived the people of the most elementary civil rights. Gandhi . . . countered by calling a *hartal,* an Indian version of a one-day general strike, but something more than that. Not only would all the factories and shops close down, but everything else: schools, newspapers, restaurants, offices, courts. Indians would simply stay home, and for one day paralyze the country. The *hartal* was called for April 6. It was not as peaceful as Gandhi had urged. All over the country there were acts of violence. They were perhaps worst in Amritsar, where five Englishmen were killed, a lady missionary was assaulted, and British banks, schools and churches were attacked. Gandhi tried to reach Amritsar and quiet the mobs, but was arrested on his way and turned back. Brigadier General Reginald E. Dyer, the commanding officer at Amritsar, decided to teach the "natives" a lesson.[11]

This is the context in which the peaceful gathering of some ten thousand Indians occurred. The meeting was to protest both the savagery of British martial law and the violence of some Indian demonstrators. A poor place for a large public gathering, the site was a two- or three-acre park entirely surrounded by the walls of buildings with only a narrow alley entrance. General Dyer blocked the entrance and, without warning, had his fifty troops open machine-gun fire on the densely packed, unarmed crowd. Sixteen hundred rounds were fired in ten minutes; 379 people were killed, 1,137 wounded. Dyer did not allow Indian medics to treat the wounded.[12]

Also at Amritsar, Dyer issued his "Crawling Order," a humiliation which Gandhi thought worse than the massacre.

> As punishment for the mob's assault of the English mission-ary woman, the General issued a command ordering all Indians who had to proceed up or down the street where she lived to crawl along it on their bellies. Hundreds of venerable old Indi-ans, who had had nothing to do with the mob, who deplored its violence, lived in the street. General Dyer posted soldiers with fixed bayonets to see that they and all other Indians who had to use that street crawled with their bellies in the dust. "Like worms," Gandhi said.[13]

These events were in 1919. They were not typical of British rule in India, yet neither were they solitary instances of British brutality. Other examples could be cited as well. Arrested and imprisoned, off and on, sometimes without trial, Gandhi spent more than five-and-a-half years in British jails between 1915 and 1944. At one point some 23,000 nonviolent activists were in jails.[14] Indian independence was won in 1947—after a nonviolent campaign of more than thirty years. The point of noting all of this here is, simply, to erode the myth that the British were a sympathetic, easy target for nonviolent activists. In fact the struggle was long and difficult against a formidable warist enemy.

A similar point can be made in response to the suggestion that Martin Luther King, Jr., had a civilized, cooperative, easy adversary in his struggles for racial equality in the United States. Eugene "Bull" Connor, commissioner of public safety, Birmingham, Alabama, symbolized his city's disregard for the Bill of Rights, the Constitution, and the 1954 decision of the U.S. Supreme Court outlawing segregation in the public schools. In early May of 1963, Birmingham jails filled with demonstrators arrested during the previous week, Connor led a small army of men armed with clubs, high-pressure fire hoses, and police dogs. His intent was to scatter crowds of unarmed men, women, and children peacefully demonstrating their support for racial equality and integration. The result was brutal ugliness documented in newsreels and press photographs seen across the nation and the world, "pictures of prostrate women, and policemen bending over them with raised clubs; of children marching up to the bared fangs of police dogs; of the terrible force of pressure hoses sweeping bodies into the streets." [15] Brutality was not limited to Birmingham; again and again nonviolent activists met determined warists, sometimes the Ku Klux Klan, sometimes government officials. There were bombings, shootings, and lynchings. This enemy was hardly the civiized "nice" people suggested by those belittling the effectiveness of nonviolent direct action.

The other side of this criticism of pacifism—that nonviolence cannot be effective against truly ruthless enemies like the Nazis (or Communists in contemporary versions)—needs to be met as well. In fact even without systematic preparation, nonviolent direct action was taken against the Nazis in a number of countries. For example, during the Nazi occupation of Norway, fascist president Vidkun Quisling established a compulsory fascist youth movement and imposed a mandatory teacher's organization under the leadership of the head of the Norwegian storm troopers. Roughly three-fourths of Norway's twelve thousand teachers went on record with Quisling's Department of Church and Education, refusing membership in the organization and defying orders to promote fascist education.

The government threatened them with dismissal and then closed all schools for a month. Teachers held classes in private homes. Despite censorship, news of the resistance spread. Tens of thousands of letters of protest from parents poured into the government office.

After the teachers defied the threats, about one thousand male teachers were arrested and sent to concentration camps. . . . The Gestapo imposed an atmosphere of terror intended to induce capitulation.[16]

The schools were reopened and the teachers still at liberty were under pressure to cooperate out of fear that those already arrested would be killed. They stood firm. Concerned that he might further alienate Norwegians, Quisling finally ordered the release of all teachers. They returned home to triumphal receptions. The schools were never used for fascist propaganda.[17] Other cases of effective nonviolent action against Nazis in Denmark, Berlin, and the Netherlands can be cited as can examples of nonviolent struggle and success against fascist rule.

It would be foolish to claim that nonviolent action always succeeds against any enemy, just as it would be foolish to claim that violence always succeeds against any enemy. We must look to the evidence of history. It should be clear that the widespread belief that nonviolence "doesn't work" is a misconception grounded in ignorance or neglect of when and where nonviolent direct action has succeeded. Similarly, the widespread confidence in violent means of struggle rests on neglect of its many failures. It must be remembered that nonviolence has succeeded with little preparation and virtually no public confidence. Meanwhile violence is systematically planned, of the highest priority when investing public resources, and widely supported, yet it frequently fails to be an effective means of achieving the peaceful ends in view. The pragmatic objections to pacifism, once examined, are not decisive refutations at all.

It must be acknowledged that pacifism may or may not succeed at defeating unrestrained evil. But there is no guarantee that violence will prevail over unrestrained evil. War, by its nature, is a test of might. As such, it can never settle questions of right.[18] Rather, in war one side prevails and domination replaces the cooperation of genuine peace.

When pushed to the extreme cases, pacifist and warist alike face the test of their values. The pacifist may have to accept defeat by refusing violence, consoled only by the knowledge of having refrained from engaging in the evil means of the adversary. The warist too may have to face defeat: the moral defeat of overriding the just-war tradition of restraint, of becoming evil to prevent the triumph of the enemy's evil, and the possible military defeat of failing to prevail despite resorting to unrestrained means. Dropping moral restraint does not guarantee victory; it only guarantees that exceedingly great evil means will be used, not that good ends will result. Beyond this, the principle of supreme emergency may be abused to urge overriding just-war requirements of moral restraint. The adversary in war can be caricatured, the evils of our enemies can be exaggerated, to rationalize our own evils. And sometimes the very fact that we engage in war allows our enemies to do greater evil than may have been possible for them had we refused to oblige them by fighting. Perhaps one difference between pacifist and warist at this point is the difference between believing that something is worth dying for (pacifists and warists may often agree on this) and believing that something is worth killing for (pacifists and warists may often disagree on this).

Some critics of pacifism may grant much of what has been said to this point yet persist that "pacifism might work if enough people believed in it, but they just don't." It is probably true that pacifism would be more effective if most people were pacifists; it is also true that most people are not pacifists. But it does not follow that pacifism succeeds only if most people are pacifists. This is not only a logical error; as we saw above, history refutes the claim as well.[19] Pacifists have been effective even as a small minority.

Shifting away from the pragmatic objections to pacifism to more theoretical objections, it is sometimes claimed that pacifism is wrong because aggression is an innate feature of human nature. While making no claim to resolve the controversy among psychologists and others as to whether aggression is learned or innate, it seems safe to recognize that this is at least an open question. Humans make choices and take responsibility for many of their actions. One would have to embrace a thoroughgoing fatalism to accept this innate aggression objection to pacifism. However, to embrace a thoroughgoing fatalism is to render all ethical thought meaningless. Appeals to human nature rarely resolve theoretical disagreements. Rather, as a type of definitive utterance, they often constitute dogmatic defenses of values and attitudes.[20] We see this in defense of racial and gender bias as various claims are made about what is "natural" for blacks, women, and so on. Perhaps the best that can be said about human nature is that humans are capable of an incredibly broad range of activities, given full opportunity to exercise and develop a variety of potentialities. Certainly there is no conclusive evidence suggesting pacifism to be incompatible with being human.

Another theoretical—rather than practical—objection to pacifism is that pacifism may be self-contradictory.[21] Critics taking this view reason that pacifists claim both "violence is wrong, *and* it is wrong to resist it."[22]

According to Jan Narveson, to say that it [violence] is wrong is to say that those to whom it is done have a right not to have it done to them. . . . If we have any rights at all, we have a right to use force to prevent deprivation of the thing to which we are said to have a right. But the pacifist, of *all* people, is the one most concerned to insist that we do have some rights, namely, the right not to have violence done to us. This is logically implied in aserting it to be a duty on everyone's part to avoid violence. And this is why the pacifist position is self-contradictory.[23]

This line of reasoning fails on several counts. At best, it is telling against only the most extreme form of absolute pacifism. But even if Narveson's attack were aimed only at such formulations of pacifism, still there are problems. For, as we have seen, pacifists do not claim that it is wrong to *resist* violence. On the contrary, they claim that violence *should* be resisted. They just believe that there are strong moral grounds for preferring to do so nonviolently; that is, it is morally better to resist violence nonviolently. Further, as the pacifist continuum above allows, a pacifist even toward the more extreme segment of the range need not assert that all humans are duty-bound to avoid violence in all forms. While rare absolute pacifists may defend this claim, such a position is not necessary to maintain that war is morally wrong and that nonviolent resolutions to conflict should be developed and practiced. Finally, again as entailed by the continuum, pacifism is a moral ideal to strive for, not a requirement all must meet to be considered human. People are pacifists—morally opposed to war and disposed toward nonviolent action—to varying degrees. The wrongs opposed as well as the ends sought are judged against moral ideals as better or worse relative to possibilities envisioned. Pacifism consists of a complex range of values, not a simple rigid dogma.

No doubt there are attempts to refute pacifism other than those considered here. The goal has not been an exhaustive and definitive defense against any and all criticisms. Rather, the goal has been to make a case for the plausibility of pacifism by calling into question the most familiar objections. Just as the caricatured thug in the alley criticism rests on misconception, stereotype, and misplaced analogy due to difference in scale, many of the stock challenges thrown at pacifists can be exposed as resting on ignorance of history or confusion of concepts.

It would be reckless to pretend that pacifism can answer all challenges; it would be equally reckless to pretend that warism can do so. If the treatment of the issues given here has seemed imbalanced toward the plausibility of pacifism, biased to favor the pacifist position, reflect on the overwhelming weight of conventional wisdom and its predisposition toward warism. Most readers have spent a lifetime immersed in a culture biased against even taking pacifism seriously. Warism is among the most deeply held and least critically examined fundamental values of modern culture. Surely the context within which pacifism must be discussed, seeing the world through warist normative lenses, more than offsets any imbalance of pacifist bias here.

CHAPTER VII

IMPLICATIONS

Peace is not an absence of war, it is a virtue, a state of mind, a disposition for benevolence, confidence, justice.

—Spinoza,
Theological-Political Treatise

Warism is the norm in the modern world. Exposing and describing the cultural inclination to presume a warist attitude on the morality of peace and war makes possible the consideration of a wide range of moral positions on war, from war realism at one extreme to absolute pacifism at the other. Examining the fundamental principles of the just-war tradition and describing the varieties of just-warism allows us to understand the moral reasoning of just-warism. Through the study of the means/ends problem in the morality of peace and war and through the development of a range of pacifist views, we have

109

been able to relate warist and pacifist positions to one another. Having described a range of views along a positive peace continuum and having considered standard objections to pacifism we can turn to the implications of the moral continuum.

Certainly one important implication of the moral-continuum model of values on peace and war is that seemingly polarized and opposite positions are in fact differences in degree and not differences in kind. Warism and pacifism are not true opposites but are extreme limits within one spectrum, the range of values on restraint in war that our moral tradition calls us to respect. Toward the extreme pacifist end of the spectrum moral restraint is absolute and no war or act of war can be justified in principle, much less in fact. Toward the war-realist end of the spectrum, war is not only justified in principle but justified in fact. The range is left entirely when restraint is total on the one hand (and no act of force between people is allowed), or when there are no restraints at all on the other (and anything goes in behavior between people).

Conceiving warism and pacifism as distinguishable segments within a moral-restraint continuum has several important advantages over the artificial dichotomy of conventional wisdom. It allows us to avoid oversimplified, stereotyped, and caricatured notions of those holding various views along the spectrum. Accusations of "war mongerer" and "bloodthirsty" on the one hand, or "sell-out" and "cowardly surrender" on the other are often exaggerated attacks that help us to rationalize the evil we are about to do by going to war or to rationalize the good we risk losing by refusing to go. While the continuum model cannot claim the simple clarity of the old polarized notions of warism and pacifism, at least it is a good deal more accurate in recognizing the subtlety, complexity, and shades of gray in which most of our judgments of morality in war seem to fall.

Another advantage beyond respecting differing degrees of moral restraint is recognizing the common value tradition from which both varieties of pacifism and varieties of just-warism spring. All those along the continuum hold convictions requiring moral restraint in war; they differ in degree over how much restraint is appropriate in various circumstances. Everyone along the continuum believes that innocents must be immune from attack; there is disagreement by degree over the extent to which harm to innocents can be excused. Anyone positioned along the continuum will require knowledge and evidence to justify the use of force by one person or group to dominate another; but standards of evidence, degrees of knowledge, and justificatory criteria vary. The point is that warism and pacifism can arise from common moral concerns; in fact, as has been shown above, some variants of pacifism are argued by appeal to principles of the just-warist tradition.

Having a common value tradition and, equally important, recognizing the common appeals to identical moral principles can help to reduce the moral and intellectual distance between pacifists and just-warrists. Rather than sharpening the differences, this recognition can deepen the communication and broaden the likelihood for understanding, respect, and even agreement-making (literally, "peace") between them. This is an important step in coming to grips with one of the most troublesome and confusing features of the continuum model, namely, the overlap between the weaker versions of both just-warism and pacifism.

In sketching the segments of the continuum above, the just-war range and the pacifist range, the possibility of overlap was suggested but never developed. This was due to the need to envision each segment of the range prior to comparing the two. Now that the full continuum has been described, the shades of gray where the two meet and even overlap must be accounted for. This is no easy problem and it will not get a quick and easy solution. We are well advised to recall Wittgenstein's observation that when we have a bright light in a dark room it is not easy to say precisely where the light leaves off and the dark begins. But, he quickly adds, this is no reason to deny that we can tell light from dark. Shaded differences along any continuum offer subtlety and difficulty; the continuum on moral restraint in war is no exception.

There seem to be several ways for the weak forms of pacifism and just-warism to overlap. One mentioned above results from the *scale* of prospective wars. A given individual may well be on the warist segment of the continuum when considering a citizen soldier's use of personal weapons to defend self and family from personal attack yet at the same time be on the pacifist segment when considering the moral justifiability of any use of strategic nuclear weapons. The close proximity, near and contained presentation of evil, and its equally near and contained response is simply easier to justify, given the knowledge one must have of threats and conditions, guilt and innocence, likely collateral injury, and so on. Another clear case of overlap appears as we consider pragmatic pacifism. The reasoning may be that war is justifiable in principle and perhaps in fact as well but that the likelihood of right prevailing seems remote. Thus non-violent resistance may be adopted only because it may work where violent resistance would surely fail. This is a sort of begrudging pacifism that is genuinely in the foggy territory between the more distinctly pacifistic and waristic segments of the continuum. Still another example of the overlap comes to mind when we envision the nuclear pacifist who may believe in just war as long as moral restraints are principled and respected. Such a person may believe even a massive-scale revolution against brutal, oppressive, and exploitative rule may be warranted provided that the requirements of the principle of proportionality are strictly met, that is, provided that excessive indiscriminate death and destruction not occur. Nuclear weapons, because they fail to meet such an individual's moral standard for discrimination and proportionality, could not be used (even if only the use of nuclear weapons could guarantee victory). And of course one may be at different points along the continuum when reflecting on different wars, for example accepting many of the Allies' actions during World War II while rejecting most U.S. actions during the Vietnam war. These variations are not contradictions. Wars are complex and subtle events, not the sorts of things one must simply accept, believe in, and support for all time or reject out of hand in every conceivable form, time, and condition. There are degrees of evil to be resisted as well as degrees of scale, proportionality of means, and certainty of cause. No doubt there are other examples where variants of pacifism described above may coexist with meeting moral conditions demanded by variants of just-warism.

This overlap can provoke pacifists and just-warists alike to reject the continuum model, each taking the other to be their moral opposite and thus neither conceding the common moral ground. Ironically, caricaturing themselves and one another as moral opposites virtually guarantees no progress at resolving their moral conflicts; were each to entertain the concept of a continuum of views on moral restraint in war and respect the varying degrees of difference in their positions, the possibility of movement in resolving their differences would arise. This, in turn, would acknowledge and allow changes in degree of position as one matures morally. Just as our other values tend to change by degree throughout our lives, so our values on morality and war must admit to degrees and to change.

To this point in the consideration of the range of moral views between the extremes of war realism and absolute pacifism, no particular position along the spectrum has been explicitly earmarked and defended as the morally superior view. No doubt readers have detected the author's bias throughout (led in part by the introductory warning), but no position has been argued to be best. This reluctance to isolate a preferred view has been deliberate for several reasons. First, all that has been said above needs to be said to establish a context within which specific views may be isolated for special consideration. Second, the very nature of the context, the nature of the moral-continuum model as a scheme for relating the variety of views on moral restraint in war, itself precludes an obvious, narrow, or clearly defined position. The very strengths of the continuum model—acknowledging subtlety, complexity, and degrees of moral criteria, evidence, scale, and conditions of various wars—guarantee some vagueness about where one ought to settle along the spectrum. Finally, this very vagueness provokes tolerance and respect for serious and carefully weighed positions taken at various places on the scale. The point is not to remain aloof and avoid taking a stand; the point is to take a stand with caution after considering the range of views and relevant factors as carefully as possible. The more one understands about the relevant factors and competing perspectives on any particular war situation, the more one respects the difficulty of confidence in our moral judgments of war. This attitude seems to lead to a moral preference for views away from the extremes, to the dismay of war realists and absolute pacifists alike.

Since war is not intrinsically good, and since the very existence of a range of views requiring moral restraint in war argues against war if it is possible to avoid or minimize it, the reasonable and moral thing for anyone confronting the prospects of war to do is to attempt backing away from war realism. To fail to do so is to surrender the moral tradition and to cease to be moral concerning war. Granting the legitimacy of the moral-restraint continuum developed here, backing away from war realism—to any degree—is backing toward pacifism, even if one never quite backs into pacifism. The moral pull of positions away from both extremes is also a matter of degree. Backing away from war realism—backing toward pacifism —is described below.

The variety of pacifism having the greatest overlap with just-warism is the weakest sort of pacifism imaginable, one so weak that many stronger pacifists will not allow it in the pacifist range. It is pragmatic pacifism, the position compatible with many variants of just-warism distinguished by the conviction that violence cannot succeed in given circumstances. On this view, pacifism is adopted as a tactic that may work where violence cannot. Whereas a violent uprising to secure rights of a racial or ethnic minority may be put down quickly in certain contexts, the nonviolent resistance of slow-downs, boycotts, and strikes may succeed. Pacifism in this context is a more practical means to the desired end than the promise of warist options. We must recall that all of us appeal to nonviolent means to resolve conflict where we can; even the war realist does not declare war to resolve every disagreement. The war option is entertained when it is thought—or presumed—to be the best or only option. So even the strongest of just-warists indeed overlap with positive peace techniques regularly. This is a first step in backing away from war realism toward pacifism.

Developments in the technology of modern war have led modern cultures to grave pangs of conscience over the evolving moral tradition and its requirement of restraint in war. This can lead to further backing toward pacifism. War itself has evolved beyond personal weapons by degrees to the point that weapons of unimaginable mass death and destruction have been created, produced, and deployed in large numbers. This gradual evolution continues in the atomic age. The weapons used on Hiroshima and Nagasaki, the ultimate weapons of 1945, were of a magnitude now considered to be theatre or tactical nuclear weapons, powers of ten smaller in destructive potential than that of today's strategic nuclear weapons. One consequence of the existence of such weapons—in such numbers at a state of readiness—is that the moral restraint of the just-war tradition precludes the use of the weapons. Of course those who take nuclear weapons to be justifiable within the moral tradition argue that the value of the weapons is in their deterrent influence, certainly not in their use.

A huge body of literature has arisen in recent years consisting of various attempts to explain, justify, or condemn deterrence policy on moral grounds. The problem, of course, is that an enemy is not deterred—literally, "frightened away"—from attacking unless the threat of counterattack is real. Consequently, adversaries must convince one another that they are not merely bluffing but are prepared actually to use their respective nuclear arsenals. A number of puzzles arise: Is it moral to threaten to do what it would be immoral to do? If so, by what reasoning? If not, deterrence is itself immoral. Further, each side seems to be in the logically questionable position of thinking the other side to be simultaneously sane and insane: sane enough to know better than attack given the inevitable retaliatory attack, yet insane enough actually to use their nuclear weapons rather than merely bluff their use. The race for nuclear, biological, and chemical weapons superiority, always justified by reference to defense, has brought about weapons that by their natures are indiscriminate and disproportional. The recognition of this gross violation of fundamental moral principles guiding traditionally required restraint in war has led to technological and nuclear pacifisms. Thus the technological developments of war have provoked evolution in modern culture's thinking about moral restraint.

There is a down side to this linkage of technology with moral restraint. Some within the just-warist tradition respond not by drifting toward technological pacifism but by calling for newer technologies of greater refinement that may produce a generation of "smarter" weapons that avoid the gross violations of the principles of discrimination and proportionality. In warning of the modern drift toward war realism and the near collapse of all moral restraint encouraged by indiscriminate and disproportionate weapons and the subsequent attitude of toleration for total war, James Turner Johnson calls for a return to the integrity of the just-war tradition by the development of "more accurate, less individually destructive, less indiscriminate nuclear weapons and beyond that . . . the development and use of other kinds of weapons in place of nuclear ones."[1] This response to the disproportionate and indiscriminate weapons of current arsenals is rather like the call to replace countercity (or countervalue) targeting of nuclear weapons with countermissile (or counterforce) targeting on the grounds that destroying weapons is less wrong than destroying people; it throws something of a curve to those urging a backing away from warism. Are the moral arguments so flexible as to allow such boomerang effects, *moral* grounds for moving *towards* warism? It is at this point that the positive peace continuum comes into play.

The call of some just-warists for the development of "smarter" nuclear weapons clearly makes moral sense only within a context of a "lesser of evils" argument. Yes, it can be admitted that if we are to have weapons of unimaginable destructive power, surely there is some sense of "better" where it is meaningful to say smarter weapons are better because they are more discriminate. But here the context needs to be questioned. The context of such just-warist arguments assumes a world where peace (the absence of war) is guaranteed by constant threat of and preparation for war. It is the negative understanding of peace that provokes this reasoning, which seems to double back on itself. If peace is not the mere absence of war but the positive condition of societies orderly from within by cooperation rather than ordered from without by coercion, fear, and force, then surely smarter weapons are no more likely to bring peace than are the grossly indiscriminate and disproportional weapons now in use. War is a test of might. As such it cannot establish conditions of orderly cooperation. War can only determine domination.

An analogous argument exposes the spuriously moral grounds for preferring counterforce to countervalue targeting. It is seemingly more humane to threaten destruction of weapons rather than destruction of cities. But on further consideration it becomes clear that targeting weapons does not guarantee protection of people, since radioactive dust may drift from missile fields across food production areas to population centers. Also, counterforce targeting may have a destabilizing effect on the balance of terror since adversaries must protect their weapons to make credible their threats of retaliation, the cornerstone of deterrence. So, if enemies fear that their weapons may be rendered useless by a surprise (preemptive?) first strike, they must devise methods to protect their weapons or to multiply them to assure sufficient surviving weapons to retaliate against a possible strike. The "overkill" of current nuclear stockpiles is evidence for believing that such is the reasoning of current nuclear powers. Again we see that all of this makes moral sense only within the narrow and limited context of peace as the mere absence of war. Clearly, on a positive understanding of peace, neither counterforce nor countervalue targeting of nuclear weapons contributes toward societies orderly by internally cooperative means rather than by the force and threat of external domination. We move away from war realism not only by degrees of moral restraint in war but also by degrees of commitment to genuine, positive peace and to the means appropriate to and consistent with such cooperative order.

When the concept of peace is positive, the immorality of space weapons defense systems becomes clear. Yes, it can be admitted that within a narrow warist context of negative peace a satellite defense system providing a shield against incoming intercontinental ballistic missiles seems better—less evil—than an offensive nuclear arsenal poised for preemptive or retaliatory strike. But, again, in a broader context of positive peace it is obvious that missile defense does not resolve conflict, establish justice, and encourage cooperative order. In fact a space weapons defense system—if technically possible— may destabilize the balance of terror because a nation with effective missile defense could make offensive strikes without fear of retaliation. This, in turn, could prompt an adversary to strike first before the missile defense system is operative (a "use 'em or lose 'em" mentality). Just as in the cases of smart weapons and the counterforce versus countervalue targeting issues, the case of missile defense systems too is a narrowly limited dispute, restricted by a warist context, a negative concept of peace, and a limited-options, lesser-of-evils argument. But there is a broader context, there are positive concepts of peace, and there are options beyond the evils from which missile strategists force a choice.

Beginning to entertain the range of positions along the positive peace continuum as we weigh the likelihood of our means to bring about peace—a weighing required by just-warism as well as by pacifism—brings us a long way from the brink of war realism, beyond the center of the just-warist/pacifist overlap on the continuum. This is because war by its nature does not instill cooperative order and agreement. War, by its nature, brings destruction, death, dislocation, and disruption of conditions favorable to genuine positive peace. We continue to back away from warism by degrees and begin to back into stronger varieties of pacifism as we seize this failure of any war. At this point the prospect of positive peace becomes the focus rather than concentrating merely on avoiding war. Now precluding war takes precedence over preparations to win dominance.

Preventing war by preparing for positive peace is morally preferable to maintaining an uneasy negative peace by preparing for and threatening war. Societies orderly by internal, cooperative control are morally preferable to societies ordered by domination, fear, force, and threat—morally preferable both from the perspectives of the citizens within the various societies and from the perspectives of those outside. Perhaps the moral preference rests on the value our tradition places on stability; perhaps it rests on fairness, respect for rights, justice, or some combination of these. Perhaps it rests on consistency between the values a nation cherishes and their means of interaction with other nations. Whatever the source of the moral preference, it certainly is central to the tradition within which this study has taken place.

The very notion of restraint in war—common to all positions along the full continuum in varying degrees—puts the burden of proof on going to war and on how the fighting is done. These are the activities in need of justification. The moral presumption should be to peace, positive peace, rather than the pervasive presumption to warism and negative peace. Recognizing the grip that warism has on culture may be the most formidable task of genuine peacemaking for the foreseeable future because it is warism that blocks evolution toward more pacifistic societies. Only occasionally will individuals back into the most absolute pacifist position; the cultural predisposition to warism confines most of us to a narrow range of options toward the war-realist end of the scale. This brings us full circle and we end this consideration of a moral continuum on war and peace where we began, confronting warism.

The normative lenses of warism, the spectacles through which we in modern culture tend to see and interpret all that happens, turn out to be as much like blinders as lenses because they restrict our vision to a narrow range of options. Nietzsche once said that, if the only tool you have is a hammer, everything begins to look like a nail. Under such conditions it is pretty hard to resist hammering. Analogously, if the only vision we have is warist and the only tools we build are weapons, everything begins to look like conflict and it becomes hard to resist warring. Unless we see a wider value perspective than the warist, we will not envision the options before us. But to see more widely we need to acknowledge and remove the blinders.

Peace education is a minute, struggling, but growing segment of contemporary education. The dominant presumption of warism has made it difficult for peace education to establish itself as a legitimate discipline devoid of the image of mere anti-militarist propaganda. Some scholars call themselves peace educators while others within the traditional disciplines are reluctant to be so labeled; they may be sympathetic with genuine peace research but afraid of the stigma that goes with the label. Those scholars interested in applying their professional training and skills to peace issues face a monumental task. Education at all levels must confront warism just as racism, sexism, and ageism have begun to be confronted across disciplines and curricular programs. There must be recovery of neglected history, consideration of the full range of moral choices concerning peace and war, acknowledgment of the narrow restrictions imposed by negative concepts of peace, and there must be more serious, systematic, and legitimized study of positive concepts of peace. Preparing for war in an effort to prevent war and preserve the *status quo* must be distinguished from preparing for peace in an effort to encourage cooperation and preclude the resort to war. Unless such issues are entertained routinely across all educational endeavors of culture, the disposition to warism will continue to drive us toward war realism and prevent progress toward positive peace. Easing the grip of warism may be unlikely, but, then, racial integration in the public schools, abolition of slavery, and women holding public office, all were exceedingly unlikely not long before they became realities. People imagine, work for, and sacrifice for important goals even if they are never achieved. To the wonder of many, unlikely goals are sometimes reached.

While education is crucial, peace educators cannot bear the burden of the cultural failure to see beyond warism. Scholars in the more traditional disciplines must explore the relevant warist/pacifist issues of their fields just as feminist scholarship has been undertaken by academics in all fields and as racist claims have been tested by research in all disciplines. It is remarkable how low peace research is among government and foundation priorities. The moral continuum here may prove useful in eroding warist obstacles to taking peace positively if only because it recognizes gradual variations among views within a single moral tradition rather than encouraging the polarized views. Peace research and study need not lead to any conversion experiences; it would be surprising were they to do so, despite popular fears.

The sort of awakening needed to become aware of warism and to do something about it may be like the alcoholic's coming to grips with personal addiction. The prospect is unlikely yet pivotal and unpredictable. Particular events sometimes stun or scare an addict sufficiently for denial to break down. Perhaps an unlikely person or incident will capture the imagination of enough of the general public to precipitate a cultural confrontation with its own warism. There was a glimmer of this in the early 1980s as the Nuclear Freeze movement gathered momentum. But again a negative focus—no more nuclear weapons—left supporters clear on what they were against but unsure of what they were for. Within a warist context the burden of proof is always on those inclined away from warism; after all, they challenge the *status quo* and threaten dominant beliefs. A positive vision must accompany such threats to offer something to replace what is challenged.

The development and defense of a moral-continuum model for understanding the range of ethical positions between war realism and absolute pacifism is an ambitious undertaking. It provides a somewhat visionary and sweeping overview of various positions on the morality of peace and war. It does so at the expense of a fuller, more detailed account that might follow each issue wherever it may lead at the risk of muddling the overview. Respect for the subtlety, complexity, depth, and breadth of factors relevant to moral judgment concerning war may come from either approach, overview or detailed study of specifics. Such respect may prompt caution, patience, and tolerance for thoughtful positions on these issues, regardless of the perspective taken. If those at all points along the continuum are made to bear the burden of proof equally without a cultural predisposition to warism, perhaps fallibility or epistemological pacifism will emerge as we admit our ignorance. It is hard to justify acts of death, obliteration, and domination that cannot be reversed; it is impossible to do so without secure knowledge of the relevant factors. But it is just such secure knowledge that seems to elude us in an era of mass media, mass destruction, and massive populations. War cannot be justified by reference to what is not known.

No doubt there are implications of the moral continuum on peace and war beyond those described here. Perhaps the reader will explore them as well as develop, correct, and extend these ideas. Backing away from warism, backing toward pacifism, needs all the help it can get.

AFTERWORD

A HISTORY OF THE IDEA
OF PACIFISM

If it is asked whether the human race at large is progressing
perpetually toward the better, the important thing is not the
natural history . . . but rather the moral.

—Immanuel Kant,
"An Old Question Raised Again"

Within a warist context, that is, within our own cultural context,
sketching the history of pacifist thought is tracking reasons for moral
opposition to war and tracing grounds for morally preferring the
conditions of positive peace. The effort here is not to delineate past
events of pacifist failures and successes at resolving conflict, struggling against oppression, and defending the good life by nonviolent means. That is an important history, one especially needed to
answer the pragmatic objections to pacifism considered in Chap-

ter VI above; but it is not the history we must examine here. Rather, the effort here is to sketch highlights of the history of the *idea* of pacifism, a moral history of the idea that humans should aspire to harmonious living and reject war. As a sketch of highlights, this is not intended as an exhaustive account but as a general overview of developments in moral restraint and alternatives concerning war.

As was seen in the chapters above, contemporary versions of pacifism often begin as criticisms of war. Such is also the case in the history of pacifist thought. And just as contemporary pacifism arises within a pervasively warist context, so the idea of pacifism emerges within the broad and deep warism of ancient cultures.

Going back to the ancient Greeks we find the warist context now familiar. Heraclitus, an influential pre-Socratic thinker of the turn between the sixth and fifth centuries B.C., considered war to be "the father and king of all."[1] He took strife or conflict as a fundamental source of all nature. What harmony there was in nature was fleeting, the transient product of natural tensions. Heraclitus was not alone in accepting war as a basic fact of nature. The ancient Greeks generally took war for granted as natural and inevitable.

The Peloponnesian War from 431 to nearly 400 B.C. between democratic Athens and oligarchic Sparta provided the backdrop for important historical, dramatic, literary, and philosophic reflections on morality and war. The war was not approved at the time by the best writers of Athens who had to live through it. Thucydides' history of the war makes clear his judgment that it was a needless war of rival ambitions where both sides were to blame.[2] One episode is particularly telling. The people of Melos, an island in the Aegean Sea, wished to remain neutral in the conflict between Sparta and Athens. Commenting on Athens' advancing despotism, Thucydides puts defensive words in the mouths of the Athenians as they explain themselves to the people of Melos:

You and we both alike know that in the discussion of human affairs the question of justice only enters where there is equal power to enforce it, and that the more powerful exact what they can, and the weak grant what they must. . . . Your subjection will give us an increase of security, as well as an extension of empire.[3]

Thucydides thus characterizes the Athenian position as the most extreme warism, to the brink of war realism. He has the Athenians continue:

For of the gods we believe and of men we know, that by a law of their nature, wherever they can rule they will. This law was not made by us and we are not the first to have acted upon it; we did but inherit it, and shall bequeath it to all time, and we know that you and all mankind, if you were as strong as we are, would do as we do.[4]

Having thus justified themselves by setting justice aside, the Athenians proceeded to destroy Melos. In Thucydides' account, "the Athenians put to death all who were of military age and made slaves of the women and children."[5]

Clearly the early ancient Greek notion is that war is a natural and inevitable extension of political strength. In his account of the civil war in Corcyra, one of the strongest indictments against war ever written, Thucydides notes that while lust for power and gain prompt the fighting, once war begins, dire necessity takes over as cause for brutality. "War is a hard master, and most men grow like the lives they lead."[6] Thucydides both exposes the dominant warist outlook of the ancient Greek world and begins the critical examination of the outlook.

Afterword

The greatest of ancient Greek dramatists contributed to early anti-warism during the Peloponnesian War. One of the most poignant and moving dramatizations of the suffering of innocents in war is Euripides' *The Trojan Women*. Veiled as a historical account of the suffering of the vanquished Trojans hundreds of years prior to its production, the play was performed the year after Melos had been sacked (C. 415 B.C.). The early audiences could not have missed Euripides' critique of Athenian warism. The great comic playwright Aristophanes also wrote and produced his biting anti-warist satire *Lysistrata* during the Peloponnesian War. In the play, Lysistrata (literally, "the peacemaker") is determined to band Theban, Spartan, and Athenian women together in a vow to have nothing to do with the men until their senseless war is ended. The resulting alienation of affection leads to hilarity while prompting anti-war reflections among audiences (then and since).

Beyond these glimmers of ancient Greek anti-warism there are the beginnings of developing the idea of moral restraint in war. Cicero refers to the Amphictyonic Council, whereby twelve leading Greek tribes unite on an equal basis for the purposes of caring for Delphi (the religious center of the ancient world) and observing rules of battle. This is the earliest known European council to attempt limiting cruelty in war.[7] Plato too outlines grounds for restraint in battle.

Plato provides perhaps the earliest complete and systematic theoretical account of war in a section of his *Republic*. Beyond arguing for the necessity of restraint in battle, Plato sketches ideas on the nature of positive peace. The *Republic* takes as its point of departure the notion that humans live best in cooperative community. Plato recognizes that no individual is self-sufficient. He speculates that society itself is founded on human interdependence and he has his Socrates sketch a society in which people share goods and services with one another to mutual satisfaction, meeting basic needs in a simple life without luxury. The people "feast with their children, . . . hymn the gods and enjoy each other, bearing no more children than their means allow, cautious to avoid poverty and war. . . . They live at peace and in good health and when they die at a ripe old age they bequeath a similar life to their offspring." [8] While Socrates considers such a society "the true city, like a healthy individual," he is pressed to examine a luxurious city (he calls it "fevered"), one dedicated to an unlimited acquisition of wealth. What he finds is that the society built on a relentless drive for wealth is the origin of war. [9]

The culture based on wealth requires a guardian class of watchdog warriors, censorship, eugenics, government lies, and the abolitions of family and private property. Such a society inevitably plunges into war. While there is disagreement among scholars over Plato's own ideals concerning social structure, two of his points on war are very clear. [10] First, war originates in an unlimited thirst for wealth. Second, war is best avoided; if not avoided, war must be restrained. Plato's primary concern is for restraint in war among Greeks:

> Now, I said, the city you are founding is Greek, is it not? — It must be.
> So your citizens will be good and civilized? —Yes indeed.
> And will they not love Greece? Will they not consider Greece to be their own? Will they not share the religion of the other Greeks? —Very much so.
> They will therefore consider their differences with Greeks, their kindred, as civil strife and will not call it war? —They will not.
> They will then quarrel as people who one day will be reconciled? —Certainly.
> They will therefore chasten their foes in a friendly spirit; they

will not punish them with enslavement and destruction. They are chastizers, not enemies at war. —Quite so.

Being Greeks, they will not ravage Greece, they will not burn the houses, nor will they maintain that all the inhabitants of each city are their foes, men, women and children, but only a few, those who caused the quarrel. For all these reasons, as the majority are their friends, they will not ravage the country or destroy the houses. They will carry their quarrel to the point of compelling those who caused it to be punished by those who were guiltless and the victims of it.

I agree, he said, that this is how our citizens must behave toward their enemies.[11]

While Plato does not extrapolate this restraint of cruelty in war beyond Greek enemies, he does outline the grounds for such extension of the argument: proportionality, and immunity of innocents. This is an early and systematic backing away from war realism; morality *is* relevant to war and requires restraint in war. The just-war tradition begins to emerge alongside war realism.

The fragmentation among city-states in the south of Greece assisted consolidation and conquest by Alexander the Great. But the widest military domination Europe had ever experienced swallowed the Greek world within the Roman Empire. From the end of the second century A.D. until the fall of Imperial Rome at the close of the fifth century, the empire was constantly at war, often along the frontiers and occasionally among rivals within. Ironically, this mighty military power was faced with early Christianity, whose spirit in the minds of its most devoted followers carried pacifism to the extreme of nonresistance—this despite fierce persecution of Christians at the hands of the Romans.

Controversy over Christianity and pacifism is virtually unending from the early days of the church to the present. Jesus' own words are quoted for and against varieties of pacifism. But whatever the convictions of Jesus, the *idea* of the moral superiority of peace and of a harmonious human family did emerge among early Christians. The extremes of the moral continuum on the ethics of war exist side by side during the early stages of the Roman Empire.

The extreme pacifism of the early Christian church was based both on gospel passages and on Jesus' own non-resistance to those who condemned him. After Emperor Constantine's declaration of tolerance to Christianity (in 313 A.D.) and after his own conversion, the church lost its pacifist disposition. As F. Melian Stawell puts it, the church conquers the empire only to be captured by its captive.[12] Before Constantine, Christians may not serve in the military under the emperors. After the alliance of empire and church, soldiers convert and Christians may fight in just wars.

The teachings of Augustine on just war are adopted by the early church. The code of war was that of Plato and Cicero with Christian additions. Jesus' words, "resist not evil," were interpreted to require an inward disposition to love that did not preclude killing. It was not actions that were right or wrong but attitudes; the point was to avoid hate. Killing and love could go hand in hand for Augustine because salvation, not the life of the body, was of extreme importance. The destruction of the body may even benefit the sinner. War must have a just intent, to vindicate justice and restore peace. War must be justly fought, without wanton violence, looting, massacre, and atrocities. And war must have right authority—the emperor determines when a war is just.[13]

Pacifism was for the most part dormant from the time of Constantine until reforming sects like Anabaptists and Mennonites in the sixteenth century. There are only isolated examples of anti-warism during the interim, and they are held by those described to be heretics by the dominant ecclesiastical authorities. The clergy were exempt from military service, but others were required to fight. The wars among Christians during the period were among the worst in Europe. The reemergence of pacifist thought occurs with rationalist and protestant revolt against the "senselessness and cruelty of trying to establish harmony by bloodshed," that is, by revolt against the crusades and the later wars to expand territory among princes of Europe.[14] "The crusade which originated in the middle ages differs from the just war in several respects. The cause is more than just, it is holy. . . . The authority of the prince is not necessary. The war may be fought under the authority of God or His representatives on earth."[15] From the early church to the middle ages, Christian values on war had moved from extreme pacifism and non-participation through reluctant participation in just war to the eager and hearty participation in the crusades.[16]

The crusades began in the dual aim of uniting the church and defeating the new civilization of Islam. They failed on both counts. Christendom was fragmented as wars against the Moslem world gave rise to East-West wars among Christians. And Islam itself advanced into Europe while the enmity between the two civilizations endured. Anti-warist thought was for the most part dormant while "the glory of medieval Christendom finally exploded into a galaxy of little Christendoms, the great national monarchies from which the pattern of modern Europe began to emerge."[17] By the early sixteenth century powerful political leaders claimed their own "divine" authority and power, adding medieval crusading zeal to the authority of the sovereign determination of when war is just.

Perhaps the most articulate critic of warism to emerge during the Renaissance was Desiderius Erasmus. He detested war. His critique is exemplary of the intellectual, emotional, and humanistic spirit of the time in which he was such a giant figure. In the *Complaint of*

Peace (1517) Erasmus asks simply, "Who is there that does not think his own cause just?" This undercuts the basis of just-warism because it rejects the notion that the sovereign can legitimately determine the justice of war.

> We have borrowed much from the laws of the Caesars. . . . Wishing to perfect our work we twist the teachings of the gospel to suit it. Roman law allows us to counter force with force and press our own claims to the utmost. . . . It glorifies war, provided it be just, and by definition it is just provided the prince declares it to be so, although the prince may be a child or a fool.[18]

In response to the argument that war is lawful because force is lawful in punishing wrongdoers, Erasmus points out that "in the courts a man is condemned and suffers according to law" while "in battle each party treats the other as guilty."[19] In the process of criticizing the warism of his time, Erasmus uses pacifist arguments from several points along the continuum including concern for the suffering of innocents as well as pragmatic concerns about whether war pays. "If you cannot have the mind of a statesman, you might at least show the sense of a shopkeeper." Erasmus is convinced that it costs more to subdue towns than to build new ones. Meanwhile, his contemporary rival, Luther, mocked pacifist thought as naive and retained the war realism of old: "War is in itself Godlike, and as natural and necessary to the world as eating and drinking."[20]

Along with the fragmentation of Christendom and political rivalries of the sixteenth century came rapid development in the techniques of war. The discovery of gunpowder and the inventiveness that characterized its use opened new possibilities for acts of war. Guns were objects of beauty, fortifications a normal part of town planning, and military virtues of courage, obedience, and strength became lauded in a revitalized cult of war. For the Renaissance humanism of Erasmus, force is brutish and reason is human; it is thus preferable to resolve conflict by arbitration and not by war. Humanism tries to undermine the cult of war by cultivating disgust for war through satire.[21] The *Praise of Folly*, the *Complaint of Peace*, and several of the colloquies of Erasmus show his wit while bluntly exposing the brutal underside of war.

The age of the Enlightenment brought protests and pleas against the religious wars and simple power struggles that had persisted in Europe. No matter the causes of the carnage, people were sick of it. A mood of peace and a spirit of reason prevailed among social and political theorists and a great many plans for European and world peace were brought forth. War was seen as a problem and internationalism was the solution. There had been suggestions of federation and arbitration to resolve conflicts between nations before; Sully, minister of Henri IV of France, and William Penn, founder of Pennsylvania, are two notable proponents of an institutionalized assembly of sovereign princes of Europe. But the various players were far too nationalistic to accept an organized Europe to which each nation and each prince would be subject. The need to preserve a balance of power was made the excuse for expanding forces and dominion at the expense of neighbors, playing off every nation against every other.[22]

Immanuel Kant's "Idea for a Universal History from a Cosmopolitan Point of View" (1784) is exemplary of Enlightenment internationalism. The view is based on both reason and prudence. The greatest problem for the human race, according to Kant, is the achievement of a universal civic society. Humans achieve their highest development only within society, more specifically, that society with the greatest freedom, where freedom is limited only as it must be for consistency with the freedom of others. Although we are enamored with boundless freedom, experience shows us that humans cannot live long together in wild freedom. Nature forces us to make at first inadequate and tentative arrangements for civility; "finally, after devastations, revolutions, and even complete exhaustion, we come to that which reason could have told us at the beginning and with far less sad experience, to wit, to step from the lawless condition of savages into a league of nations."[23] However fantastic the idea may seem (and Kant tells us it was laughed at by Rousseau), states must come to the decision that individuals were reluctantly forced to take in the past, namely, "to give up their brutish freedom and to seek quiet and security under a lawful constitution."[24]

On Kant's model, humanity—the individual as well as the species —is evolving from more brutish toward more rational behavior. While the evolution is uneven with setbacks as well as strides forward, the general drift is away from violent imposition of will toward arbitration, compromise, and cooperation. In "Perpetual Peace" (1795), Kant offers a more detailed account of human progress toward internationalism especially as it involves Europe. By trial and error we learn individually and collectively to constrain our own freedom out of respect for the freedom of others. The laws we follow free us because we legislate them for ourselves. Experience confirms what reason determines. "Reason, from its throne of supreme moral legislative authority, absolutely condemns war as a legal recourse and makes a state of peace a direct duty, even though peace cannot be established or secured except by a compact among nations."[25] Without international tribunal, war alone is the means to resolve differences. "But by war and its favorable issue in victory, right is not decided."[26] So Kant condemns war on practical as well as moral grounds.

Toward the end of "Perpetual Peace" Kant shows particular sensitivity to the victims of conquest. Noting that originally no one had more right than another to any particular part of the earth, Kant records numerous

> inhospitable actions of the civilized and especially of the com-
> merical states of our part of the world. The injustice which
> they show to lands and peoples they visit (which is equivalent
> to conquering them) is carried by them to terrifying lengths.
> America, the lands inhabited by the Negro, the Spice Islands,
> the Cape, etc. were at the time of their discovery considered
> by these civilized intruders as lands without owners, for they
> counted the inhabitants as nothing.[27]

While Kant does not explicitly address the recourse that such victims may be justified in taking, he underscores the practical and moral failure of war and regards international law as "indispensable for the maintenance of the public human rights and hence also of perpetual peace."[28] Unless nations as well as individuals subject themselves to principles of order that respect the rights of their peers and give up claims to moral superiority, disorder will prevail and the arbitrary and awful condition of war will continue.

Toward the middle of the nineteenth century Adin Ballou, leader of the New England Non-Resistance Society, developed pragmatic pacifism to a level previously unknown. Seizing the warist's most common justification for violence, self-defense, Ballou says, "If it be the true method, it must on the whole work well. It must preserve human life and secure mankind against injury more certainly and effectively than any other possible method. Has it done this? I do not admit it."[29] Ballou goes on to cite the death tolls from history, millions slain in war, most in the name of self-defense. To preserve those lives that were preserved at such a staggering cost itself renders life a thing of doubtful value to Ballou. If only a few thousand or even a few million had perished, if innocence and justice and right had always triumphed, if aggression, violence, and injustice always had been defeated, if gradually the world had come out of barbarity by these self-defensive wars into a condition of peace and justice, if self-defensive violence had deterred aggression, perhaps then we could believe that self-defensive war was justifiable. But history demonstrates that we are no better off, rather that we are worse off for having used self-defensive violence.[30]

Ballou takes the consequentialist to task. When wars are taken to be justifiable and justified, they are so as means to some end. Ballou simply reminds us of what the results have been. His is not a principled pacifism that forbids violence out of respect for human rights or divine command; he simply calls on the consequentialist to examine the empirical evidence of the results of justifying violence by appeal to self-defense. Rather than proposing definitive grounds for pacifism, Ballou undermines the principle justification of warism. Pacifism is defended indirectly by exposing the failure of the consequentialist justification of war.

The most prominent pacifist thinker in the late nineteenth and early twentieth century was Leo Tolstoy, the Russian novelist and social reformer. His was an extreme religious pacifism in the tradition of the kenotic Christ. "Kenotic" is a Greek word that means emptying. The notion is that Jesus as the Christ was not a being equal with God; not a thing to be grasped, Jesus *emptied* himself. This provides the ideal of total self-abnegation. For Tolstoy, we are children of God. As such, we must renounce and humble ourselves. Christ does not call us to suffer; but we must not resist evil and this entails suffering. Tolstoy's pacifism calls for a renunciation of civil authority as well as war because the state and society themselves rest on violence.[31] By the beginning of the twentieth century the extremes within pacifism are contesting with the full range of warism as humanity approaches the most horrifying wars of all time.

With his little essay, "The Moral Equivalent of War," William James makes a notable contribution to pacifist thought in 1910. What James points out is that, despite the widespread evidence of the evil and stupidity of war, exposing irrationality and horror has no effect on dissuading people from supporting war. The budgets of all nations show that war taxes are the only ones we never hesitate to pay. Why?

James argues that pacifism must get beyond anti-warism to replace war with a positive alternative as inspiring and exciting as the commitment to war has been. The point is that war entails glory, sacrifice, supreme importance, risk, opportunity for heroism, in sum, a psychological attraction that alternatives to war simply lack. However sensible an international forum for arbitration of conflict between nations may be, it does not capture the popular imagination to serve the psychological function of the commitment to risk all in battle over noble causes. James himself is a pacifist who sees war to be evolving to the point that it is absurd and impossible due to its own monstrosity. Yet, James grants, a peaceful world cannot be built without what he calls the martial virtues—intrepidity, contempt of softness, surrender of private interest for the good of all, obedience, physical fitness, responsibility, hardihood, discipline, civic honor— all these traditional virtues of dedicated military personnel must be employed for peace rather than for war.

Rather than resist these martial virtues, James advocates channeling them in a constructive way. Life is hard and people must work and suffer to sustain life. But by mere accident of birth and opportunity, some people have lives of ease while others have only toil and pain and inferiority imposed on them. James proposes replacing the war system with a youthful, conscripted army enlisted to confront planetary conditions with the purpose of evening out imbalance and injustice.

> To coal and iron mines, to freight trains, to fishing fleets in December, to dishwashing, clothes-washing, and window-washing, to road-building and tunnel making, to foundries and stoke-holes, and to the frames of skyscrapers, would our guilded youths be drafted off, according to their choice, to get the child-ishness knocked out of them, and to come back into society with healthier sympathies and soberer ideas. They would have paid their blood-tax, done their own part in the immemorial human warfare against nature; they would tread the earth more proudly.[32]

Needless to say, James' moral equivalent did not capture the imagi-nation of the public. World War I did. Perhaps this verified a more cynical comment of James from the beginning of the very same essay:

> Every up-to-date dictionary should say that "peace" and "war" mean the same thing, now *in posse,* now *in actu.* It may even reasonably be said that the intensely sharp *preparation* for war by the nations *is the real war,* permanent, unceasing; and that the battles are only a sort of public verification of the mastery gained during the "peace" interval.[33]

James leaves us wondering whether the war system may have done irreparable harm—making itself inevitable by its complete grip on culture before, during, and after actual military conflict—or whether war has made itself obsolete through its own technological advance.

Afterword

World War I shattered the optimism of internationalists and of those who had thought growing economic interdependency between nations would preclude massive armed conflict. At the same time the horrors of the war reinforced anti-warist convictions. Necessity challenged cynicism as the League of Nations was formed to promote collective security. The League enjoyed some early success but the indifference and independence of major powers left it weak and ineffective by the early 1930s. World War II, obliteration bombing, and the creation and use of nuclear weapons, all contributed to a second effort at internationalizing guarantees of peace and security. But again the reluctance of major powers to be subjects of a strong United Nations left the world without reliable means to curb war. The most effective international alliances were forged to make war against other alliances. Various pacifists enjoyed remarkable successes on domestic struggles during the twentieth century, working for women's suffrage, child labor laws, and civil rights as well as resisting involvement in war. Jane Addams, Mohandas Gandhi, and Martin Luther King, Jr., are among the most widely known contributors to positive peace. Yet internationally the war system remains intact.

One explanation for the persistence of war, offered between the world wars by John Dewey, seizes the seeming natural inevitability of war as the focus of his critique. According to Dewey, the argument for the natural necessity of war

> convinces us of the folly of striving to eliminate war by agencies which leave other institutions of society pretty much unchanged. History does not prove the inevitability of war, but it does prove that customs and institutions which organize native powers into certain patterns in politics and economics will also generate the war pattern. The problem of war is difficult be-

cause it is serious. It is none other than the wider problem of the effective moralizing or humanizing of native impulses in times of peace.[34]

Dewey's insight is that while war is not inevitable in itself it may be the inevitable by-product of political and economic injustice. This reminds us of the subtlety and complexity of the problem, makes us wary of simple solutions, and increases respect for those pacifist activists who have helped create positive peace.

Although it is difficult—perhaps even foolish—to predict the historical direction of pacifism during our own time, it may be worthwhile to speculate. It seems that one lesson of our time is that, no matter how complicated we think things are, they often have ways of turning out to be even more complicated than we had thought. Pacifism may turn out to have many more nuances of meaning than are suggested here, and the same may be said for just-warism. Gandhi and King—perhaps the most widely known pacifists of this century—use pacifist arguments from across the spectrum, absolute to pragmatic pacifism. The increasing discussions of technological and nuclear pacifism and the growing understanding that moral principles from the just-war tradition can prompt pacifist positions on existing military options should broaden and deepen the dialogue on morality and war. Perhaps even the cultural drift toward war realism, the willingness in this century to resort to total war, and the recognition that the superpowers' weapons are less and less likely to achieve political goals will have stark and sobering effects on our once glib warism. Peace will not break out, but a backing away from warism may begin.

When we attempt an overview perspective on the history of the idea of pacifism we see many high and low points but we also see a general drift from the war realism of the ancient world toward the increasing necessity for authorities to provide moral justification for preparations and acts of war. Today's leaders cannot get away with embracing a crass war realism as did Athenian leaders of the fifth century B.C. Beyond this, we see an increasing recognition that peace is secured by justice, that war is prevented by fostering conditions of internal, cooperative order more than by threat of forced domination. Post-World War II military failures underscore this. Finally, the study and practice of nonviolence is expanding knowledge of positive peace. Such backing toward pacifism is not backing into pacifism but it is movement in the right direction.

NOTES

Chapter I

1. One of my most disturbing experiences as a young father was when my then four-year-old daughter announced upon her return from nursery school that she planned to be a nurse. When asked whether she had considered being a doctor she said, "No Daddy. *Boys* are doctors; *girls* are *nurses*." At that moment, nothing could have been more obvious to her or less obvious to me.

2. Iredell Jenkins, "The Conditions of Peace," *The Monist* 57, no. 4 (Oct. 1973): 508.

3. Edwin A. Burtt, "Philosophers as Warriers," in *The Critique of War*, ed. Robert Ginsberg (Chicago: Henry Regnery, 1969), pp. 30–42.

4. Warren E. Steinkraus, "War and the Philosopher's Duty," in *The Critique of War*, ed. Ginsberg, p. 3.

5. *Ibid.*, p. 6.

6. Michael Walzer, *Just and Unjust Wars* (New York: Basic Books, 1977), p. 21.

7. John Dewey, *Problems of Man* (New York: Philosophical Library, 1946), p. 186.

8. Jane Meyerding, "Reclaiming Nonviolence: Some Thoughts for Feminist Womyn Who Used to Be Nonviolent and Vice Versa," in *Reweaving the Web of Life: Feminism and Nonviolence*, ed. Pam McAllister (Philadelphia: New Society, 1982), pp. 12–13.

9. Walter W. Skeat, *A Concise Etymological Dictionary of the English Language* (Oxford: Clarendon Press, 1882; rpt. 1965), pp. 378 and 375 respectively.

10. Mohandas K. Gandhi, "The Doctrine of the Sword," *Non-violent Resistance*, ed. Bharatan Kumarappa (New York: Schocken, 1951), pp. 132–134.

11. Carl von Clausewitz, *On War*, trans. Michael Howard and Peter Paret (Princeton, N.J.: Princeton University Press, 1976), pp. 75–89.

12. Skeat, *Concise Etymological Dictionary*, p. 599.

13. Jan Narveson, "Pacifism: A Philosophical Analysis," *Ethics* 75, no. 4 (July 1965), reprinted in *War and Morality*, ed. Richard Wasserstrom (Belmont, Calif.: Wadsworth, 1970), pp. 63–77.

14. *Ibid.*, p. 63.

15. *Ibid.*, p. 71.

16. Cheyney C. Ryan, "Self-Defense and Pacifism," in *The Ethics of War and Nuclear Deterrence*, ed. James P. Sterba (Belmont, Calif.: Wadsworth, 1985), p. 46.

17. John Dewey, *Human Nature and Conduct* (New York: Henry Holt, 1922), p. 3.

18. For a useful discussion of how warist-biased language bars open dialogue on peace issues see Thomas Merton's "War and the Crisis of Language," in *Critique of War*, ed. Ginsberg, pp. 100–117. For a survey of academics' views on pacifism, see George W. Hartmann, "The Strength and Weakness of the Pacifist Position as Seen by American Philosophers," *Philosophical Review* 53 (March 1944): 125–144.

19. Karl Popper, *Objective Knowledge* (Oxford: Oxford University Press, 1972), p. 266.

Chapter II

1. See Thucydides, *History of the Peloponnesian War*; Hobbes, *Leviathan*; Machiavelli, *The Prince*; Clausewitz, *On War*; and so on.

2. Carl von Clausewitz, *On War*, trans. Michael Howard and Peter Paret (Princeton, N.J.: Princeton University Press, 1976), p. 76.

3. *Ibid.*

4. This account of the just-war tradition generally follows James Turner Johnson (*Can Modern War Be Just?* [New Haven, Conn.: Yale University Press, 1984]) and Michael Walzer (*Just and Unjust Wars*).

5. Walzer, *Just and Unjust Wars* (New York: Basic Books, 1977), p. 21.

6. Augustine in Johnson, *Can Modern War Be Just?*, pp. 50–51.

7. Johnson, *Can Modern War Be Just?*, p. 25.

8. *Ibid.*, p. 5.

9. Walzer, *Just and Unjust Wars*, p. 146.

10. *Ibid.*, pp. 152–159.

11. Johnson, *Can Modern War Be Just?*, p. 16.

12. *Ibid.*

13. Jenny Teichman, *Pacifism and the Just War* (Oxford: Basil Blackwell, 1986), p. 41.

14. Walzer, *Just and Unjust Wars*, p. 254.

Chapter III

1. Antony Flew, "Ends and Means," in *The Encyclopedia of Philosophy*, ed. Paul Edwards (New York: Collier-Macmillan, 1967), Vol. II, p. 508.

2. *Ibid.*, p. 510.

3. *Ibid.*

4. I was reminded of this point by President Reagan in his speech to an American Legion Convention, Aug. 23, 1983. Portraying the peace movement as naive and simplistic, the President's basic message was that his ambitious arms buildup was not inconsistent with a quest for peace. "Peace

is an objective, not a policy," Reagan said. See George Skelton, "Reagan: Peace Activists Are Naive," *Minneapolis Star and Tribune*, Aug. 24, 1983, p. 1A and 8A.

5. John F. Kennedy, Inaugural Address, Jan. 20, 1961.

6. Thomas Merton, "War and the Crisis of Language," in *The Critique of War*, ed. Robert Ginsberg (Chicago: Henry Regnery, 1969), p. 108.

7. *Ibid.*

8. *Ibid.*, p. 112.

9. Flew, "Ends and Means," p. 508.

10. John Hersey, *Hiroshima* (New York: Alfred A. Knopf, 1946; Bantam ed., 52nd printing, 1981), p. 1.

11. Joseph C. Kunkel, "Right Intention, Deterrence, and Nuclear Alternatives," *Philosophy and Social Criticism* 10, nos. 3–4 (Dec. 1984): 143–155.

12. Joseph C. Kunkel, "Just-War Doctrine and Pacifism," *The Thomist* 47, no. 4 (Oct. 1983): 510.

13. *Ibid.*, p. 502.

14. *Ibid.*, p. 509.

15. Michael Walzer, *Just and Unjust Wars* (New York: Basic Books, 1977), pp. 61–62.

16. Hanna Arendt, *On Violence* (New York: Harcourt Brace Jovanovich, 1969), p. 36.

17. Sara Ruddick, "Remarks on the Sexual Politics of Reason," in *Women and Moral Theory*, ed. Eva Kittay and Diana Meyers (New York: Rowman & Allanheld, 1987), p. 240.

Chapter IV

1. Ronald B. Miller, "Violence, Force, and Coercion," in *Violence: Award Winning Essays in the Council for Philosophical Studies Competition*, ed. Jerome A. Shaffer (New York: David McKay, 1971), pp. 30–33.

2. Leo Tolstoy, "Address to the Swedish Peace Congress in 1909," in *The Kingdom of God Is Within You*, trans. Aylmer Maude (Oxford: Oxford University Press, 1936; rpt. 1951), p. 586.

3. I am not claiming that Kant was an absolute pacifist but that one could base an absolute pacifist conviction on one interpretation of the categorical imperative.

4. Martin Benjamin, "Pacifism for Pragmatists," *Ethics* 83, no. 3 (April 1973): 196.

5. Jan Narveson, "Is Pacifism Consistent?" *Ethics* 78, no. 2 (Jan. 1968): 148.

6. Tom Regan, "A Defense of Pacifism," *Canadian Journal of Philosophy* 2, no. 1 (1972): 86. I must note that the title of Regan's paper may be misleading; while he defends pacifism against Narveson's allegation of inconsistency, he rejects pacifism on moral grounds.

7. *Ibid.*

8. Martin Luther King, Jr., *Why We Can't Wait* (New York: Mentor, 1964), p. 30.

9. For a helpful discussion of the relations between violence, force, and coercion see Miller, "Violence, Force, and Coercion," pp. 11–33.

10. See Thomas Hobbes, *Leviathan*, Pt. I, chap. 10.

11. Mohandas K. Gandhi, *The Story of My Experiments with Truth*, Pt. IV, chap. 29, reprinted in *Non-Violent Resistance*, ed. Bharatan Kumarappa (New York: Schocken, 1951), p. 3.

12. Mohandas K. Gandhi, *Hind Swaraj or Indian Home Rule*, chap. 17, in *Non-Violent Resistance*, ed. Kumarappa, p. 17.

13. Jonathan Schell, *The Fate of the Earth* (New York: Alfred A. Knopf, 1982), pp. 129–130.

14. John C. Ford, "The Morality of Obliteration Bombing," *Theological Studies* 5 (1944): 261–309 reprinted in *War and Morality*, ed. Richard Wasserstrom (Belmont, Calif.: Wadsworth, 1970), p. 15.

15. *Ibid.*, in *War and Morality*, ed. Wasserstrom, pp. 23–24.

16. *Ibid.*, pp. 35–36.

17. *Ibid.*, p. 15.

18. Schell, *Fate of the Earth*, p. 100.

19. This model was suggested to me by Bill Gay.

20. Aldo Leopold, *A Sand County Almanac* (Oxford: Oxford University Press, 1949; rpt. Ballantine, 1970), p. 262.

21. Thomas Powers, "Nuclear Winter and Nuclear Strategy," *Atlantic Monthly* 254, no. 5 (Nov. 1984): 58. In addition to his excellent summary Powers provides bibliographic references to the major studies.

22. That many people did so during the civil rights struggles of the 1960s was disturbing to Martin Luther King, Jr. See King, *Why We Can't Wait*, p. 152.

Chapter V

1. Anonymous author, *Report from Iron Mountain*, quoted in Hanna Arendt, *On Violence* (New York: Harcourt Brace Jovanovich, 1969), p. 9.

2. Michael Walzer, *Just and Unjust Wars* (New York: Basic Books, 1977), p. 274.

3. *Ibid.*

4. Mulford Q. Sibley, "Concluding Reflections: The Relevance of Non-Violence in Our Day," in *The Quiet Battle*, ed. Mulford Q. Sibley (Boston: Beacon, 1963), p. 1.

5. *Ibid.*, p. 362.

6. *Ibid.*, pp. 359–362.

7. Iredell Jenkins, "The Conditions of Peace," *The Monist* 57, no. 4 (Oct. 1973): 511.

8. Sibley, "Concluding Reflections," pp. 363–364.

9. Jenkins, "Conditions of Peace," p. 516.

10. *Ibid.*, pp. 516–517.

11. *Ibid.*

12. *Ibid.*, pp. 517–519.

13. E. F. Schumacher, *Small Is Beautiful: Economics As If People Mattered* (New York: Harper & Row, 1973; Perennial Library ed., 1975), p. 84.

14. Craig K. Ihara, "In Defense of a Version of Pacifism," *Ethics* 88, no. 3 (July 1978): 369.

15. Jenkins, "Conditions of Peace," p. 520.

16. Albert Camus, *Neither Victims nor Executioners* (Chicago: World Without War, 1972), p. 53.

17. Gene Sharp, *The Politics of Nonviolent Action* (Boston: Porter Sargent, 1973), p. 3.

18. See the discussion of collectivist pacifism in Chapter IV above.

19. Sharp, *Politics of Nonviolent Action*, pp. 4–5.

20. *Ibid.*

21. Martin Benjamin, "Pacifism for Pragmatists," *Ethics* 83, no. 3 (April 1973): 197.

22. Richard Barnet, *The Economics of Death* (New York: Atheneum, 1970), p. 5, quoted in Benjamin, "Pacifism for Pragmatists," pp. 200–201.

23. Benjamin, "Pacifism for Pragmatists," p. 201.

24. Gene Sharp, *Making the Abolition of War a Realistic Goal* (New York: Institute for World Order, 1980).

25. *Ibid.*, pp. 7–8.

26. *Ibid.*, p. 9.

Chapter VI

1. For a thorough treatment of the history of nonviolent action see Peter Brock, *Pacifism in Europe to 1914* (Princeton, N.J.: Princeton University Press, 1972); Brock, *Pacifism in the United States from the Colonial Era to the First World War* (Princeton, N.J.: Princeton University Press, 1968); Brock, *Twentieth Century Pacifism* (New York: Van Nostrand Reinhold, 1970); *The Quiet Battle*, ed. Mulford Q. Sibley (Boston: Beacon, 1963); Gene Sharp, *Power and Struggle*, Pt. I of *The Politics of Nonviolent Action* (Boston: Porter Sargent, 1973); and *The Power of the People*, ed. Robert Cooney and Helen Michalowski (Culver City, Calif.: Peace Press, 1977).

2. Sharp, *Power and Struggle*, p. 76.

3. Gene Sharp, "Making the Abolition of War a Realistic Goal," in *Power and Struggle*, p. 5.

4. *Ibid.*

5. *Ibid.*

6. Hanna Arendt, *On Violence* (New York: Harcourt Brace Jovanovich, 1969), p. 53.

7. Michael Walzer, *Just and Unjust Wars* (New York: Basic Books, 1977), pp. 332–333.

8. Narveson, "Pacifism: A Philosophical Analysis," in *War and Morality*, ed. Richard Wasserstrom (Belmont, Calif.: Wadsworth, 1970), pp. 68–69.

9. William L. Shirer, *Gandhi: A Memoir* (New York: Simon & Schuster, 1979), p. 31.

10. *Ibid.*, p. 32.

11. *Ibid.*, pp. 32–33.

12. *Ibid.*, pp. 33–34.

13. *Ibid.*, pp. 34–35.

14. Ved Mehta, *Mahatma Gandhi and His Apostles* (Harmondsworth, Eng.: Penguin, 1976), pp. 152–154.

15. Martin Luther King, Jr., *Why We Can't Wait* (New York: Mentor, 1964), p. 100.

16. Sharp, *Power and Struggle*, p. 87.

17. *Ibid.*, p. 89.

18. Jenny Teichman, *Pacifism and the Just War* (Oxford: Basil Blackwell, 1986), p. 109.

19. The logical error is the fallacy of affirming the consequent.

20. This point was suggested, in another context, by Tom Moody.

21. See also page 14 above.

22. Narveson, "Pacifism: A Philosophical Analysis," in *War and Morality*, ed. Wasserstrom, p. 75.

23. *Ibid.*, pp. 72–73.

Chapter VII

1. James Turner Johnson, *Can Modern War Be Just?* (New Haven, Conn.: Yale University Press, 1984), p. 40.

Afterword

1. Fragment 53.

2. F. Melian Stawell, *The Growth of International Thought* (London: Thornton Butterworth, 1929; rpt. 1936), pp. 14–15.

3. Thucydides, *Thucydides*, Vol. II, trans. Benjamin Jowett (2nd ed.; Oxford: Clarendon Press, 1900), p. 169.

4. *Ibid.*, p. 173.

5. *Ibid.*, p. 177.

6. *Ibid.*, p. 19.

7. Stawell, *Growth of International Thought*, p. 21.

8. Plato, *Republic* 372b, 372d.

9. *Ibid.*, 373e.

10. See Duane L. Cady, "Individual Fulfillment (Not Social Engineering) in Plato's *Republic*," *Idealistic Studies* 13, no. 3 (Sept. 1983): 240–248.

11. Plato, *Republic* 470e–471b.

12. Stawell, *Growth of International Thought*, p. 35.

13. Roland H. Bainton, *Christian Attitudes Toward War and Peace* (Nashville: Abingdon, 1960), pp. 92 and 96–97.

14. Stawell, *Growth of International Thought*, p. 74.

15. Roland H. Bainton, "Congregationalism and the Puritan Revolution from the Just War to the Crusade," in *Studies on the Reformation* (London: Hodder & Stoughton, 1964), p. 249.

16. *Ibid.*, p. 248.

17. Windass, Stanley, *Christianity vs. Violence* (London: Sheed & Ward, 1964), p. 59.

18. Erasmus, in Stawell, *Growth of International Thought*, p. 88.

19. *Ibid.*, p. 88.

20. Luther, in Stawell, *Growth of International Thought*, p. 96.

21. Windass, *Christianity vs. Violence*, pp. 60–63.

22. Stawell, *Growth of International Thought*, p. 113.

23. Immanuel Kant, "Idea for a Universal History from a Cosmopolitan Point of View," in *On History*, ed. Lewis White Beck (Indianapolis: Bobbs-Merrill, 1963), pp. 16 and 19.

24. *Ibid.*, p. 19.

25. Immanuel Kant, "Perpetual Peace," in *On History*, ed. Beck, p. 100.

26. *Ibid.*

27. *Ibid.*, pp. 103–104.

28. *Ibid.*, p. 105.

29. Adin Ballou, in Richard Wasserstrom, "On the Morality of War: A Preliminary Inquiry," in *War and Morality*, ed. Wasserstrom (Belmont, Calif.: Wadsworth, 1970), p. 91.

30. *Ibid.*, p. 92.

31. Bainton, *Christian Attitudes Toward War and Peace*, p. 195.

32. William James, "The Moral Equivalent of War," in *War and Morality*, ed. Wasserstrom, pp. 12–13.

33. *Ibid.*, p. 6.

34. John Dewey, *Human Nature and Conduct* (New York: Henry Holt, 1922), p. 109.

Index

Index